Dr. Burns' Prescription for Happiness*

*Buy Two Books and Call Me in the Morning

Also available in Large Print
by George Burns:

How to Live to Be 100—or More

Dr. Burns' Prescription for Happiness*

GEORGE BURNS

*Buy Two Books and Call Me in the Morning

G.K.HALL &CO.
Boston, Massachusetts
1986

Published in Large Print by arrangement with
G. P. Putnam's Sons.

British Commonwealth rights courtesy of
Arthur Pine Associates.

G. K. Hall Large Print Book Series.

Set in 18 pt Plantin.

Library of Congress Cataloging in Publication Data

Burns, George, 1896–
   Dr. Burns' Prescription for happiness.

   (G. K. Hall large print book series)
   "Buy two books and call me in the morning."
   1. Happiness—Anecdotes, facetiae, satire, etc.
2. Large type books.   I. Title.   II. Title:
Prescription for happiness.
[PN6231.H35B87   1986]   818'.5402   85-24744
ISBN 0-8161-3942-3 (lg. print)

Contents

Foreword

*H*ERE I AM writing another book. It's my fifth book, but my first foreword. All my other books I just started with Chapter I. I don't know whether I'm more excited about writing my fifth book or my first foreword. In fact, I couldn't sleep last night. I'm not sure if it was the fifth book, the first foreword or the Mexican dinner I had.

I did a lot of research on forewords, and the trick of a good foreword is that it shouldn't be too long a foreword or too short a foreword. Another thing, it shouldn't be too good a foreword, or it'll make the book look bad. The smart thing would be for me to write a bad foreword. But it's not easy to sit down and try to write a bad foreword. I don't know how so many people have managed to do it. But then a lot of them just specialize in writing forewords; they don't write the rest of the book. No wonder they can write bad forewords— they've had a lot of practice. I haven't. Don't forget, this is my first foreword. And if it turns out to be good, it might be my last.

Wait a minute, there's something disturbing me. My friends Jim and Henny Backus recently wrote a book and asked me to do the foreword, and I wrote all this same stuff for them. I feel terrible. I just feel awful. My conscience is bothering me. Either that or it's that Mexican meal again. I don't know what to do. I can't use this foreword now. But then again, why not? If it was bad enough for their book, it's certainly bad enough for mine.

Hollywood Center Studios
Hollywood, CA.
May 20, 1984

Hollywood Center Studios.

Canyon Hotel, Palm Springs.

Preface

As LONG AS I'm doing my first fore-word, I figured I'd do my first preface, too. But I had a problem. I didn't know the difference between a foreword and a preface. So I decided to ask my editor and publisher, Phyllis Grann. After all, she's a very intelligent lady, a college graduate and very well respected in the publishing business. I called her on the phone and said, "Phyllis, what's the difference between a foreword and a preface?"

She said, "Foreword starts with an F, preface starts with a P."

Now that she straightened me out I can go ahead with this preface. I feel great about it. Either that, or I've finally gotten over that Mexican meal.

I'm so confident right now about this preface that I'm going to put it in not only before I read my book, but before I write it. You've got to be willing to gamble a little to be a good author—take a few chances. After I read the book, if the preface doesn't fit, then I'll write a new book.

Canyon Hotel
Palm Springs
May 22, 1984

Introduction

YOU'RE PROBABLY ASKING yourself, "Why is he writing another book?" It's not healthy to talk to yourself, so I'll tell you. Actually, I was in the middle of writing a new country song, "There Are Cobwebs on My Mailbox 'Cause I Never Hear From You," when the phone rang. It was my publisher with an idea for another book, called *Dr. Burns' Prescription for Happiness*.

"Don't you want to do another book? The last one was so successful, this one will sell a million copies," she told me. "Will your song do that well?"

I looked at the song again, and now I'm doing another book. That's the way I am—quick decisions. Some people worry—did they do the right thing, did they do the wrong thing? Not me—I never look back. Boy, have I made mistakes.

So this book is going to be *Dr. Burns' Prescription for Happiness*. I don't know how I became a doctor so fast, especially since I never got past the fourth grade. But the publisher is giving me a nice advance, so if she wants me to be a doctor, I'll be a doctor. It might be fun. I can't wait to touch somebody's pulse.

Happiness is something everybody wants. We all pursue happiness, but catching it is the problem. It's not easy to come by; you don't go into a store and say, "I'll have a pound of happiness."

What is happiness, anyway? Where do you find it? If you find it, how do you hang on to it? If you can't find it, where do you look for it? If you lose it, how do you get it back? Why am I asking you these questions? I'm the doctor. I just looked it up in the dictionary. It says, "Happiness is the enjoyment of pleasure." So I looked up pleasure. It said, "See Happiness."

Happiness is different things to different people. To some it's having great wealth, lots of possessions; to others it's having nothing. To some it's being in love; to others it's being married. A while back there was a popular song that decided "Happiness Is a Thing Called Joe." I always thought that happiness was a thing called Trixie . . . or Margie . . . or Gina . . . or La Verne . . . or her mother. I'm not too fussy.

Happiness is a state of mind, it comes and

goes. You can't be happy twenty-four hours a day . . . twenty-three maybe. You deserve an hour for lunch. It's also elusive, contradictory and inconsistent. Blondes don't always have more fun, not everyone adores canned salmon, and if what pleases some didn't make others miserable, you wouldn't have the world divided into "Smoking" and "No Smoking."

There are no rules, no guaranteed formulas, and if you—Wait, it just occurred to me if that preface I did doesn't fit, I don't have to write a new book, I'll just write a new preface. Hey, I better make a note of that. Why am I making notes? I can read it, I just wrote it.

Where were we? Oh yes, I was telling you about happiness. But what's the rush? This is just the introduction, we have lots of time for that. Stick around. We'll have a few laughs. Here and there you may come across something that makes sense to you. And two or three or you may even find that I helped you. As doctors go, that's not a bad percentage.

Carlos' Cantina
Tijuana
May 23, 1984

Carlos' Cantina, Tijuana.

About the Author

NOW THAT I'VE introduced the book, I should probably introduce myself. It's always nice to know where your author is coming from. Right now your author is coming from Beverly Hills. Originally he came from Pitt Street on the Lower East Side of New York. Now Pitt Street is right next to Ridge Street, and Ridge is right next to Attorney, then comes Clinton, the Norfolk, Suffolk, Essex. This might mean nothing to you, but knowing that kept your author from getting lost.

And I wasn't always George Burns. I was born Nathan Birnbaum, and when I was a kid they called me Nat. That's not all they called me. Of course, in those days I wasn't your author, I was just starting out in vaudeville and I did all kinds of acts.

I was Harry Brown of BROWN & WILLIAMS, Singers, Dancers, & Rollerskaters. I was Joe Pierce of PIERCE & GIRLIE, The Whirlwind Dancers. I did a seal act, CAPTAIN BLUE & FLIPPER. I was Captain

Blue. I was Jack Harris of DUNLAP & HARRIS. I was the straight man and Dunlap was the comedian, who also turned out to be a straight man. We were the first comedy team who ever had two straight men. I was Barney Darnell . . . Maxey Kline . . . Willy Bogart . . . Lily Delight (I was also a female impersonator).

I remember I was sitting in a small-time booking office, and a theater manager came in and said, "Where can I find Maurice Stinelli?" I said, "I'm Maurice Stinelli." I thought I was.

I changed my name every week; I couldn't get a job with the same name twice. It's not that I was committing any crime, although some of the audience who saw my act might dispute that. Fortunately, in those days not many people saw my act. I don't want to knock myself, but I considered it a successful engagement if I could get through my opening song.

There are a few things I should tell you here, things I'm sure you'd want to know about your author. I must admit, for example, my left leg is an eighth of an inch longer than my right leg. But then again my right leg is an eighth of an inch shorter than my left leg. So it balances.

I drink coffee with my right hand, and I smoke cigars with my left. But I talk with both hands. Incidentally, unlike my legs, my hands are both the same size. Although I do have one ingrown cuticle. I'm ashamed to tell you which finger.

What else can I tell you? Oh yes, my sleeping habits. I average about eight hours of sleep a night. When I travel it could be less, depending on how hard the pillow is, or what's going on in the next hotel room and whether or not I've been invited.

I'm also very fussy about my teeth. I brush them twice a day, and I use dental floss religiously. But not the waxed dental floss—I can't stand that wax. This is my fifth book and I've never revealed that fact before. But these days when you write you're expected to tell everything. And there's one more thing I've never revealed before. I can't bring myself to use a plastic shoehorn—it must be metal.

I could go on, but other people see you differently that you see yourself. So here are the opinions of some of my closest friends about your author:

BOB HOPE:
"The first time I saw George Burns on the

stage I could see he had what it takes to become a big star—Gracie Allen."

WALTER MATTHAU:
"I did *The Sunshine Boys* with George, and everything I know about acting I learned from Jack Lemmon."

JOAN RIVERS:
"Since I met him ten years ago there hasn't been a day that I didn't think of George Burns. And I didn't think of him again today."

STEVE ALLEN:
"I was very excited about George's last book because I thought it was."

MILTON BERLE:
"I have to say this about my friend George. He looks just the same today as he looked forty years ago—old."

CAROL CHANNING:
"I never make a move without calling George Burns, and I just don't know what to say about him here because his line is busy."

DANNY THOMAS:
"Even when he was a kid George had lots of charisma. Then he started dating girls and the charisma cleared up."

JOHNNY CARSON:
"George Burns has been on my show twenty or thirty times, or maybe more. How can you turn down a guy that age?"

DON RICKLES:
"When you talk about George Burns you're talking about a living legend . . . well, a legend, anyhow.

JACK CARTER:
"There's one thing you can say about George, he wears well. But so do my army shoes."

RED BUTTONS:
"George Burns, what a man. He read in the paper that it takes ten dollars a year to support a kid in India. So he sent his kids there."

PHYLLIS DILLER:
"I've had a crush on George for years. He's my kind of guy. He's handsome, he's suc-

cessful and he's breathing."

BOB NEWHART:
"The way George Burns sings, even E. F. Hutton doesn't listen."

These comments turned out to be a little embarrassing, but remember they're close friends, so naturally they're prejudiced in my favor.

Well, I don't know about you, but I'm ready to start the book; that is, as soon as I get out of here. I can't understand it. All I had last night was a bowl of chili, a couple of burritos and some refried beans.

Cedars-Sinai Medical Center
Room 811
May 24, 1984

Cedars-Sinai Medical Center

I

Getting to the Bottom of It (Don't Worry, I'm Not That Kind of a Doctor)

Author fully recovered and ready for work.

BEFORE I START handing out my prescriptions for happiness, let's see if we can pin down the diagnosis. What do we know about it?

Well, for one thing, happiness is not a disease, although it can be contagious. You don't pick it up from drinking the water, it's not inherited and it doesn't seem to be confined to any one country, race or economic class. It can be seen anywhere, but probably less among the very poor. Some say it's not too common among the very rich, either, but I can't buy that one until I see more research on it.

I like to go by what I know or have personally observed. And I've noticed some interesting things about happiness. It can come on slowly, or you may suddenly break out with a dose of it—once you've had it doesn't mean you can't have it again—and what gives it to you now may not give it to you another time. I've also noticed that even though there are no telltale marks on the body, I can immediately tell when somebody has it. There's a certain look that's unmistakable.

As to what brings it on, it's been attributed to everything from winning a horserace to riding the ninth wave on a surfboard. There are those who insist that it's at its very best during sex. I think that also needs more research, and I personally volunteer for it.

Putting it all together, everything I see tells me that far from being a disease, happiness is an all-too-rare condition, of short or long duration, with wonderful symptoms and not one but many causes.

Not everyone could come up with this diagnosis. But I try to keep my eyes and my mind open. I'm always learning. In fact, I learned something from this diagnosis. I just realized that my prescriptions can't be for curing your happiness; they'll have to be for helping you get it.

II

Has Happiness Had It?

Happiness is reading a good book.

WHEN I WAS starting this book I ran into a friend of mine, Barry Lefkowitz. You don't know Barry Lefkowitz. Why would you? He's my friend, not yours. I don't know why I even mentioned his name. Let me start this chapter over.

When I was starting this book I ran into a friend of mine, and I made the mistake of telling him about it. "You gotta be kidding!" he screamed. "In 1984?! With all that's going on in the world, you're giving out prescriptions for happiness? You're dead in the water, man! Who can be happy today? It's over. It's yesterday's mashed potatoes! Why don't you give them a book on something really helpful, like *How to Build a Bomb Shelter?*"

It was very upsetting. I don't like being dead in the water. I'm not even sure I'd like it on the land. I don't know where I'd like it. I'm hard to please.

But my friend is not alone. Everywhere you go you hear the same thing—how can you be

7

happy in today's world? You can't blame them. When you look around it's not the kind of a picture my girlfriend Grandma Moses would have painted.

There's crime all over the place; people shooting people for the fun of it. There are wars going on in countries they don't even know the names of. There are terrorists taking hostages, blowing up embassies and sending letters that go off in your face. There are friendly nuclear warheads stacked across the street from enemy warheads. There are laser weapons that can blind you, nerve gases that can wipe out entire cities—and there are even worse things, but I won't mention those. It's not that I don't want to scare you—I don't want to scare myself.

The thing is, you don't have to let all this get you down. There are ways to fight it. Listen to Old Doctor Burns here; he's got a few tips for you.

First of all, skip the bad parts of the newspaper: the headlines, the editorials and mostly the news. Just read the comics, the sports pages and "Dear Abby." Don't even look at your horoscope.

And don't watch the news on TV, either. Or those prime-time soaps like "Dallas" and "Dynasty," unless you can take murder, rape,

Just cut out the bad news.

Author watching a situation comedy on TV.

incest, glamorous, conniving women, adultery and a lot of rough sex. The Old Doctor knows what he's talking about—he's never missed one of those shows.

Stay away from all those situation comedies, too. I saw one last night I couldn't believe. It was about this kid who gave a birthday party for his friend who's an orphan and has leukemia. There wasn't a laugh in it. If they wanted to make it really funny, why didn't they give the kid a limp, too? If you must watch television, watch something nice and cheerful like "Andy Williams' Christmas Show," "Perry Como's Christmas Show," my specials, "Johnny Cash's Christmas Show," "John Denver's Christmas Show," my specials, "Mac Davis' Christmas Show," my specials.

Oh yeah—and don't go to parties with all those intellectuals who sit around analyzing the problems of the world. Go to parties where they talk about each other's clothes, the "in" restaurants, the latest gossip, why Princess Di is having another baby, who's sleeping with your girlfriend . . . stuff that can't hurt you.

It just occurred to me that my friend Barry Lefkowitz is going to feel awful that I mentioned his name and then took it out. Maybe

I should have left it in, he's such a good friend. But I had to take it out, it made no sense. Why am I so worried? He probably won't even read the book.

Where was I? Oh yes, I was going to say that things these days aren't all bad. The price of gas is coming down, the hemlines are going up and despite everything people are living longer today than ever before. Which is good and bad; I have a lot more relatives to deal with, but there are more people around to buy my book.

Look, there were always things to worry about. Do you think the caveman had it so good? Sometimes we were miserable—starting fires with sticks, wall-to-wall dinosaurs, and no martinis. Believe me, when a dinosaur stares at you, you can use a martini.

Everyone talks about the good old days. I happen to be an expert on them—I was there. And it's true, we didn't have today's problems. There were no highway accidents because there were no automobiles. And there was no television, no radio, no refrigerators, electric ovens or pop-up toasters. They weren't invented yet. And if they had been invented, I wouldn't have had them anyway, because as far as my family was concerned money hadn't been invented yet, either.

If it wasn't for my grandmother, we would have been in real trouble. She used to go around to all the weddings in the neighborhood whether she was invited or not. And she wore a petticoat under her skirt that had a big, deep pocket on the right side. At these weddings she'd fill that pocket full of food. When we'd see her coming home, if she tilted to the right, we knew we had something to eat. To this day I don't enjoy chicken unless it's got a little lint on it.

My father was a wonderful man, but I guess he figured after giving my mother twelve kids he'd provided enough. He was very religious. In fact, he was a part-time cantor. During the High Holidays if the cantor caught cold and couldn't sing, my father would take his place. One year it happened. The cantor got sick so my father did the singing. The following year that same cantor got sick. Instead of sending for my father they closed the synagogue. I think I inherited my voice from my father.

This reminds me of when I first saw *The Jazz Singer*, which was about a cantor, too. It was the original Broadway version starring Georgie Jessel. This cantor wants his son to follow in his footsteps, but the boy loves show business. And at the finish of the play the

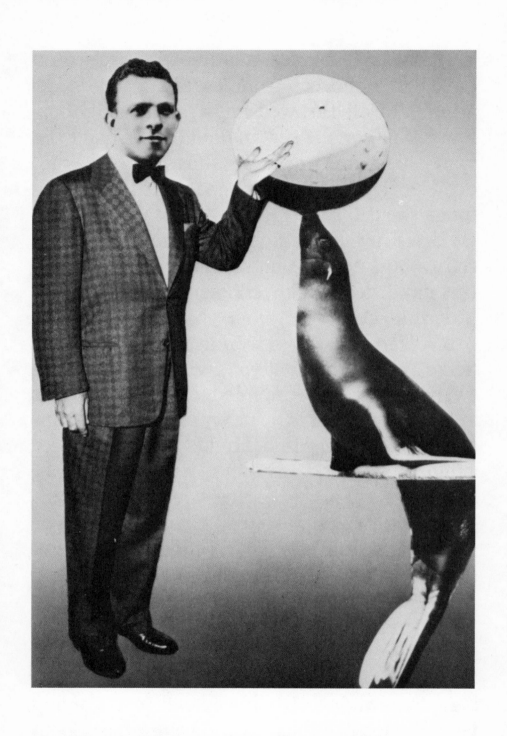

Author and partner in the "good old days."

father dies, the boy gives up show business, takes his father's place in the synagogue and before the last curtain he sings "Kol Nidre," which is a very sacred song.

I was in the audience watching, and it affected me deeply. I sat there and cried. I thought they were doing the story of my life. And after the show I went backstage with tears in my eyes to congratulate Jessel. But the doorman said, "You can't go into his dressing room, he's got his clothes off."

I said, "I've seen a naked Jew before, I just want to tell him how great he was."

The doorman whispered, "He's got a girl in there." I was shocked. I didn't think anything could follow "Kol Nidre."

Looking back at those days when I was growing up I can see now that it wasn't a bed of roses, but at the time I thought it was. Sure, there were plenty of things to be unhappy about, but nothing bothered me. I was in show business, I had orchestrations in my key, I had pictures of myself wearing a blue suit and yellow spats. I even had my own hair in those days. I was beautiful. Of course, I didn't have too many jobs, but I was ready. One time I was ready for seven to eight months. I laid off so long that my spats faded.

In those days even if you got a job there was a clause in the contract that you could be canceled after your first performance. I'll never forget once I was booked into the Farley Theater in Brooklyn. Monday morning at nine o'clock I was rehearsing my music. The manager heard my rehearsal and canceled me. I was the only actor in show business who was ever canceled before he opened.

Another time somehow I was booked into the Gem Theater on Houston Street, which was on the Lower East Side of New York. I got a contract to play three days for $15—$5 a day—and the contract had a no-cancellation clause in it.

Well, after the matinee when I came off the stage the manager was waiting for me. He said, "Look, kid, that act of yours can close my theater. You're booked here for three days for fifteen dollars. Here's the fifteen—go home."

I said, "Not me, I'm booked here for three days and I'm going to play the three days."

He said, "I'll give you twenty—go home."

I said, "All right, so you didn't like my first show. For the next show I'll change my songs. I'll open with 'Tiger Girl,' and then I'll sing 'In the Heart of a Cherry,' and then I'll do my big closing number, 'I'll Be Waiting for You,

Bill, When You Come Back from San Juan Hill.' ''

He said, "I'll make it twenty-five."

I said, "No, sir, I'm staying. I'm a performer and I can prove it. I've even got cards printed."

He said, "Okay, kid, you can stay, but give me back your key to the men's room."

I did, but that was kind of bad because that's where I was dressing. And let me tell you something. When you don't go to the men's room for three days it doesn't help your singing any. In fact, after the second day I didn't dare do my yodeling finish.

Oddly enough, for me those were happy times. And I have a hunch that fifty years from now they'll be saying, "Why can't we be happy like those lucky people in the good old 1980s?"

It's an interesting thought. I wonder if they'll really be saying that. I can hardly wait to find out.

Monday's Prescription

Dr. George Burns, H.S.
(HAPPINESS SPECIALIST)

DATE_____

NAME_____

ADDRESS_____

One Hot Tub *Monday*

Take with 1 blonde -- accompanied
by soft music and tall drink.

Repeat as desired.

If unable to get blonde, get
brunette.

If unable to get blonde or
brunette, take cold shower.

GB   ℞

Dr. Burns giving a patient a shot.

Nine Definitions of Happiness

Lists are very popular these days. There are lists on everything. And they're always ten—ten best this, ten best that. So to be a little different I decided to make my list nine. And it wasn't easy; it took me hours to figure out which one to leave out.

Anyway, here they are:

Happiness is:

1. Having a large, loving, caring, close-knit family; especially if they live in another city.
2. Hearing your proctologist say, "You can straighten up now."
3. Taking your car to the garage for a lube and oil, and getting it back with just a lube and oil.
4. Hearing your teenage kid say, "Dad, you're right." (My son Ronnie is forty-nine and I'm still waiting.)
5. Having a legitimate excuse for not attending a bar mitzvah.
6. Being stopped by a mean-looking 240-pound motorcycle cop and having him compliment you on your driving.

7. Telling your favorite joke without having Milton Berle beat you to the punch line.
8. A good martini, a good meal, a good cigar and a good woman . . . or a bad woman, depending on how much happiness you can stand.
9. Retaining your mental and physical powers despite advancing years. (I feel very fortunate. At eighty-eight I can do everything I could do when I was eighty-seven.)

Three more definitions of happiness.

III

You Can't Get There With Shortcuts Unless You're a Butcher

REMEMBER THAT SONG called "The Best Things in Life Are Free"? I sang it at the Odeon Theater on Pitt Street on the Lower East Side of New York. When I sang it I used to follow the bouncing ball. The manager at the Odeon didn't like my singing so he had the ball bounce out into the street. And when I followed it out to finish my song he wouldn't let me back in. That story isn't true. The Odeon Theater was not on Pitt Street, it was on Clinton Street.

Anyway, it was a good song and a nice thought, but it wasn't true then and it isn't true now. If a pair of jockey shorts can cost $4, how can the best things in life be free? Look, good health, a good marriage, good kids, self-respect, pride of accomplishment, they don't fall into your lap. You have to work at them a little.

It's a shame, but there are no shortcuts to happiness. Everyone's in a hurry these days. They want things prepackaged, precanned or prefabricated. It's called modern living. You go into the supermarket and buy boxes and plastic containers of artificially flavored, seasoned and colored food. Then you get into your car with the simulated leather seats and drive home to your prefabricated house. Everybody wants things instantly. Not me. I want things to last for a while. At my age if it's over too fast, I forget what it was I did, or why I did it, or whom I did it with.

It's amazing the routes some people take to get to happiness. Like drinking—and I'm not talking about drinking, I'm talking about DRINKING! The problem with that kind of drinking is, the people who do it usually don't know the condition they're in.

I remember I was on the Pantages circuit with Jack Whitehead, a monologist, and the opening act was a dancing team called The Gliding Gascoynes. And Gascoyne and Whitehead did a lot of drinking together. One night they really got bombed, and Gascoyne passed out in his dressing room. Whitehead sent for the doctor, and when Whitehead came out of the room, I said, "How's Gascoyne?"

He said, "He's really in bad shape. The doctor said to him, 'Do you see any pink elephants or green snakes?' and Gascoyne said, 'No.' And the room was full of 'em."

There have been some pretty good drinkers in show business: John Barrymore, Joe E. Lewis, Phil Harris, Dean Martin. The last time I saw Dean in a nightclub he staggered out on stage with a glass of booze in his hand, turned to his piano player and said, "How long have I been on?" It got a big laugh, but I don't think Dean drinks as much as he says he does. Nobody can drink that much. As a matter of fact, here's a true story. A woman jumped up on the stage one night, grabbed the drink out of Dean's hand and drank it. She said, "This isn't booze—you're drinking tea!" Dean looked at her and said, "Lady, you're drunker than I am." I hope I didn't just put the kid out of business.

Look, I drink a couple of martinis now and then. It's not to escape from anything—I enjoy it. If I come home at the end of the day and my help doesn't have a martini waiting for me, it's not the end of the world. It might be the end of my help, but that's a different story.

To some people it's not the drinking they enjoy, it's the ritual that goes with it. Some years ago José Ferrer moved into Beverly Hills, and one night I dropped in about nine o'clock to say hello. He asked me if I'd like a martini and I said sure. Now when I make a

Author having his daily martini.

martini I take an old-fashioned glass, fill it with ice, then fill it with gin, put in some vermouth, and in two seconds I've got a martini.

But not José. First he got a snifter glass big enough to swim in, took three jiggers of gin and slowly rolled them down the side of the glass. Then he took an eyedropper filled with vermouth and carefully rolled two drops down the other side of the snifter. Then he took one ice cube and a spoon and gently lowered it into the glass so as not to bruise the gin. Then he took the snifter glass in both hands and rocked it back and forth until the cube of ice melted. I went home at eleven o'clock and he was still making that martini.

I went back to pay him a visit three months later and he said, "George, can I make you a martini?" I said, "I haven't got time, I'm booked to play Vegas in two weeks."

Another shortcut that's being taken more and more these days is drugs: grass, acid, coke, speed, angel dust, 'ludes and heroin. Even prescription drugs like Valium, Percodan, Codeine, all sorts of amphetamines and barbiturates. People don't go to church anymore for peace of mind, they run to their pharmacy.

No one really knows how many people are on drugs these days. There are many surveys being taken, but they're unreliable—half the people taking the surveys are stoned. Our government is spending billions of dollars to put a few people into space. From what I can see the problem isn't getting people into space, it's getting them out of it. There are kids in school today on drugs. They can't have fire drills anymore—the minute a bell rings, the kids think they're being busted.

Some of our biggest athletes, the ones we should be looking up to and admiring, are users. It used to be that a good score meant you won the game by a comfortable margin. Now a good score means you made a hell of a "buy." I read about a quarterback who got caught using drugs before a game. Of course, if I had to go out there and face those 290-pound linemen, I'd probably want to be in another world, too. But what good is a drug that after you take it you can't find your fingers?

Look, I've been around a long time, and drugs have been around a long time. I don't use drugs, that's why I've been around a long time. I'm even afraid to take a laxative more than two days in a row.

When drugs became such a big thing out here on the West Coast I didn't know what they were talking about. A lot of people said they were smoking grass, so I thought I'd try it. I went out on the lawn, pulled up a handful of grass, pushed it into my cigar holder and lit it. It was nothing, but the fertilizer was murder.

I went to one of those parties without knowing it. I was hardly in the door when one of the guests came up to me and said, "George, have you got any junk on you?" I said, "No, I give it all to the Salvation Army." It was the first time I ever saw anyone with two heads look at me like I had three.

Later at dinner this attractive young girl sitting next to me leaned over and said, "George, do you ever use uppers?" I said, "What for, I've got my own teeth."

The woman on the other side of me started to laugh and said, "She's talking about those uppers and downers." I said, "Oh, 'The Uppers and Downers'? I've never seen them. Where are they playing?" They all thought I was trying to be funny. They didn't know I had never been to a party like that.

At the end of the meal out came a bowl of white power surrounded by a lot of little silver spoons. Well, I like my coffee sweet, so I put in three or four spoonfuls. The next thing I knew the host was showing me to the door. And you won't believe this—I was never invited back.

That's me at one of those parties.

33

These shortcuts to happiness all turn out to be dead ends. That's true not only of drinking and drugs, but also of gambling.

I see how you can get hooked on drugs or booze. Both are habit-forming and very difficult to give up. But compulsive gambling is something else again. How intelligent, often successful people can keep on losing and losing until they've lost everything is beyond me. I once heard a psychiatrist explain that the compulsive gambler has a subconscious desire to lose. What he really wants is not a big win, but a big loss.

I didn't believe that until the wife of a big gambler I know told me that when her husband comes home and mopes around she knows he's won a few thousand. If he comes home smiling, she knows he's lost the car or a bank account. And if he's laughing, it's time to start packing—the house is gone.

So maybe the psychiatrist was right. I do know that compulsive gamblers don't quit. This same fellow swore to me recently that he was all through—he'd promised his wife and there would be no more gambling. I said to him, "Come on, you said that same thing a dozen times."

"This time, George," he said, "it's different. I'm through gambling. I'm finished."

You can't lose gambling like this. From Going in Style *with Art Carney.*

I said, "I'll bet you ten dollars you're not through gambling." And he said, "Okay, you got a bet."

This may come as a shock to you. Jack Benny gambled. I was standing right next to him at a table in Las Vegas one night when he held the dice for three-quarters of an hour. Finally I said, "Throw 'em, already!" So he did, crapped out, lost five dollars and we had to hold *him* for three-quarters of an hour.

After a while I went to bed, but Jack stayed there and gambled all night. When I came down to the casino the next morning there he was at the same table. By then he was out ten dollars. But it didn't bother him. He figured it was still cheaper than renting a room.

Actually, when you count all the free drinks and all the cigars they gave him, he wasn't out ten dollars, he was ahead twenty dollars. Wait a minute, he had to tip all those cocktail waitresses. So he was only ahead about $19.00 . . . maybe $18.50. I don't know—I was sleeping at the time.

I play Lake Tahoe and Las Vegas a lot. In fact, I just signed a contract with Caesars for five years. They wanted to make it twenty, but I wasn't sure Caesars would be around that long. I just played Tahoe and the gambling is unbelievable. People come in by the busload and head right for the casino. They're at the tables and slot machines night and day. I was the only one who knew there was a lake out there. Even young couples who come up there do nothing but gamble all day. Sex is like the lake; nobody knows it's there. I know it's there. At my age I'm stuck with the lake.

In the dining room if you see a young attractive couple, and if the man has his hand under the table, he's counting his chips. If her hand is under the table, she's counting his chips, too. It might be fun—I wouldn't know. I haven't had my hand under a table, January 20 will be thirty-one years. But if you're interested, the lake is 192 square miles, 1644 feet deep and has 71 miles of shoreline.

It's the same thing in Vegas. The last time I was there a honeymoon couple was staying in the room next to mine. They'd been there five days. They went down and played blackjack, lost all their money and couldn't afford to get married.

I don't even know why people bring their children there. Last year a man and wife arrived and the first thing they did was put their kids in the pool. They went straight to the dice table and won forty thousand dollars. Then they took a trip around the world, came back six months later, dried the kids off and took them home. They had two of the cleanest, most shriveled-up kids you've ever seen.

The thing about gambling is you can't beat Lady Luck. I knew a girl from Cleveland, she was a stripper who called herself Lady Luck. Believe me, she didn't give anything away for free. Well, she wasn't exactly from Cleveland, she was born in Akron and moved to Cleveland. I think that was the way it went. I was sleeping at the time—no, no, you're wrong. I was sleeping alone.

Anyway, what I've been trying to say is there are no shortcuts to happiness. I don't know any shortcuts to anything. If I did, this chapter wouldn't be so long.

He must be a good doctor—he's got a stethoscope.

Tuesday's Prescription

Dr. George Burns, H.S.
(HAPPINESS SPECIALIST)

DATE_____

NAME_____

ADDRESS_____

Tuesday

For attacks of worry and anxiety--
1 hour brisk morning walk--
Stop 20 minutes to smell flowers.

May augment by singing in
shower, whistling in elevators
and dancing in the dark.

If still no relief, try mineral
oil.

GB

℞

IV

As the Saying Goes . . .

THERE ARE A lot of highly respected, time-honored sayings and expresions about happiness, and may I tell you something, we'd be just as well off without them. They all sound good, but when you stop to analyze them they don't make any more sense than the ones on the other subjects.

For example, how many times have you heard someone say, "He's happy as a clam"? You've probably said it yourself. I know I have. "Happy as a clam." Who knows how happy a clam is? He might be miserable. He might be very bored stuck in that same shell all his life. And maybe he can't stand all that sand up his bivalves. Yeah, bivalves—look it up like I did.

Or you'll hear: "I'm in a bad mood. I got up on the wrong side of the bed this morning." A bed is a bed. What's the difference which side you get up on? And if it bothers you to get up on one side, get up on the other. Personally, I don't care which side of the bed

I get up on. I'm happy just gettng up.

"Happy is as happy does." That's one I've been hearing all my life and I still don't know what it means. I wouldn't even put that in a fortune cookie.

And what about this piece of advice: "Let a smile be your umbrella." I tried that once. I had pneumonia for six weeks and shrunk a $450 suit.

And here's another beauty. "Laugh and the world laughs with you." Try going around laughing all the time. Not only won't the world laugh with you, you'll end up doing your laughing in a straitjacket.

They make it sound so simple and so easy. Who are "they"? If they're so smart, why don't "they" identify themselves? "Laugh and the world laughs with you." When I do my next TV special, instead of hiring writers and a lot of guest stars, why don't I just stand there and laugh for an hour? It would be very entertaining; I'd be a riot. It's too bad I don't know who comes up with these great sayings. I don't know who to thank.

Now, "Money can't buy happiness"—that's not bad. The Rockefellers, the J.P. Morgans, the Fords, they're not happy—they just look happy. I can go along with the idea that just having money doesn't guarantee that you'll be happy. But then they tell us that "Money is the root of all evil." From just not buying happiness, money suddenly becomes the worst thing in the world. I mean, isn't that going pretty far? If money is the root of all evil, what happened to adultery and jealousy, and spoiled meat and all the other bad stuff?

But okay, let's say they're right: "Money is the root of all evil." Then we hear, "A fool and his money are soon parted." What are they talking about? If money is so evil, shouldn't it be, "A wise man and his money are soon parted"? And another thing, how does a fool get money in the first place? I know some fools who have a lot of money, but they won't tell me how they got it, and I won't tell them.

These sayings drive you crazy. What are you supposed to go by: "Look before you leap" or "He who hesitates is lost"? The other day I was crossing an intersection in Beverly Hills and stopped in the middle to decide whether to leap or hesitate, and a kid hit me in the rear end with a bicycle.

"Pride goeth before a fall." Wrong. A banana peel goeth before a fall. "You can't judge a book by its cover." What else are you going to judge it by? Suppose this book had a cover that said "Holy Bible." Wait, that's not such a bad idea. The Bible sells pretty good. It's the only thing I know that gets into more hotel rooms than Lily Delight.

"A penny saved is a penny earned." Big deal. You can put that one with "An ounce of prevention is worth a pound of cure." That was fine during the Depression when you could get a steak for a nickel. Today I don't know where you could get even a quarter of an ounce of prevention for a pound of cure.

I say we're better off ignoring all these one-line gems. So we won't make a stitch in time and save nine. We'll only save eight. And maybe we can't make a silk purse out of a sow's ear, but look at the fun we'll have trying.

Maybe you don't agree with me. Maybe you think this whole chapter was a waste of time. Well, so do I. But then again, it's not as though you laid out twenty or thirty dollars for the book. Don't forget—as that wise old saying goes, "You get what you pay for."

The Nine Happiest Men I've Known

1. JACK BENNY—
    That is, when he was with me. He never stopped laughing. If I said anything, he fell on the floor. If I didn't say anything, he fell on the floor. His suits were always at the cleaners.

2. ME—
    When I made Jack, one of the world's greatest comedians, laugh. He made me feel like I was nine feet tall. In fact, he had me so convinced I almost became a basketball player.

3. BOB HOPE—
    Bob has a knack for making the best of a bad situation. While we were all here with our families every Christmas, there was Bob, stuck in some camp 10,000 miles from home with only a Marilyn Monroe, Raquel Welch, Loni Anderson, assorted starlets and beauty queens to pass the time with. But Bob didn't complain, he was happy doing it for his country.

168 years of Happiness.

4. MILTON BERLE—
It's no accident Milton Berle's so happy. He's got a reason, a good reason. I know, because I have the locker next to his at our club. Some of us get applause when we go onstage; Milton gets applause when he goes to the shower.

5. DON RICKLES—
Contrary to his image, Don is one of the nicest, most cheerful, contented and well-adjusted guys I know. But if he asks me once more to marry his mother, I'm going to sew up that big mouth of his.

5. HOWARD COSELL—(alternate)
Like Rickles, Howard is not what you see. He's a modest, soft-spoken, gentle soul who never criticizes and loves everything and everybody. He's also five inches taller with his shoes off and has a beautiful head of hair under that thing he's wearing.

6. AL JOLSON—
Why wouldn't he be happy? He was the world's greatest entertainer in just about everyone's opinion, including his.

7. CALVIN COOLIDGE—
Of all the Presidents I've known, Calvin Coolidge had the best sense of humor. I thought he was even funnier than Herbert Hoover.

8. BENJAMIN FRANKLIN—
Ben was really something. He was always flying kites. He'd keep four or five kites on a string. That's not all he kept on a string. You don't think he spent all his time writing *Poor Richard's Almanack*, do you?

9. JULIUS CAESAR—
There was a guy who appreciated good entertainment. If Julius liked you, there was nothing he wouldn't do for you. If he didn't, he'd throw you to the lions. I've got claw marks to prove it.

Spencer Tracy and Maurice Chevalier with two great actors.

The Nine Happiest Women I've Known

The Wives and Girlfriends of Milton Berle!

The doctor's caddy.

Wednesday's Prescription

DR. GEORGE BURNS, H.S.
(HAPPINESS SPECIALIST)

DATE_____

NAME_____

ADDRESS_____

Wednesday

No prescription today.

Doctor is on golf course.

R

V

Is Aggravation a No-No?
Yes-Yes!
(It's Not Easy to Think
of a Funny Title)

DO YOU KNOW the difference between irritation and aggravation? You don't? Well, I'm going to tell you. The other day I was sitting by my pool getting a little sun when the phone rang. I ran into the house, picked up the phone and a voice on the other end said, "Is Harry there?" So I said, "You've got the wrong number," and went back to the pool. Twenty minutes later the phone rang again. I ran in, grabbed the phone, again the same thing—"Is Harry there?" I said, "Listen, you've got the wrong number!" A half hour later the same thing happened. "Is Harry there?" That's irritation.

Now this is aggravation! Again the phone rang, and this time I heard, "This is Harry. Were there any messages for me?"

That didn't really happen to me. That's a story that was going around a few years ago. I told it because after that weak title I thought it would be nice to start off with something really funny, because the chapter's about irritation and aggravation, and because there happens to be a difference between the two. Ordinarily a comedian doesn't have to give three reasons for telling a funny story. But I'm not just a comedian now. In case you've forgotten, I'm also Dr. Burns—Old Dr. Burns.

Anyway, to me irritation is something that makes your skin red. Aggravation is paying the pharmacy $12.50 for something to cure the irritation, and when you get the bottle home you can't open it.

Right there we may have one of the major aggravations of 20th-century America. Nothing opens. Jars are impossible. Peanut butter, jam, pickles, those lids are on to stay. My thumb has never been the same since I tried to twist a new jar of peanut butter open. They tell you to put warm water over it and pound the lid. I tried that with a jar of mayonnaise. I pounded the lid on the kitchen sink, broke the jar, had mayonnaise all over the sink, but the lid stayed on.

In restaurants sugar used to be in a bowl. Pepper and salt were in shakers. Now it's all wrapped in cellophane. The crackers are wrapped, the mustard, the ketchup, the butter—the only thing that isn't wrapped is the check. Maybe you can get all that stuff open with your fingers, but I can't. I have to bite it and my teeth aren't that great. I'd like to save them for the food.

What I can't get over, they're even doing it with fertilizer. Not too many fertilizer bags come in cellophane, but try to undo the thick string they've woven through that heavy paper. Come on, it's fertilizer, it's not the Romanoff jewels! Let us at it!

Prescriptions are the worst of all. The regular bottles were bad enough, but when they started making them child-proof, did it ever occur to them they were also making them senior citizen-proof? Jack La Lanne couldn't open one of those bottles, what chance have I got? I realize we don't want the kiddies munching on our nitroglycerin pills, but if I'm having a heart attack I don't want to stand there for twenty minutes trying to figure out the combination.

There are a lot of other aggravations that we have to put up with these days. Just one by itself may not be too bad, but when you put them all together it spells MOTHER—No, no, that's a song I used to sing. What I meant to say was when you put them all together you begin to feel like Don Knotts looks. And when you're that upset and uptight you're anything but happy.

Probably the biggest single cause of tension

headaches in America, and maybe in the world, is everyday city traffic. There's nothing like two hours of bumper-to-bumper on a Los Angeles freeway to send your blood pressure up fifty points. And that's when you're out there for pleasure. How about when you're a half hour late to your job, or an important meeting, or a doctor's appointment to check your blood pressure? And how do you calm yourself down when the greatest date of your life is ten miles away and you're moving two inches a minute? By the time you get there she's married and has two kids.

Some of our best inventions can be the most aggravating. Computers, for example. They save time, but has anybody ever added up the hours millions of people spend every day trying to correct the errors made by those computers? They shouldn't bother. Computer errors don't get corrected; they're there forever. There's a $185 charge that was added by mistake to one of my credit card statements. I've pointed it out to them, they've acknowledged it, but every month it's there. And the interest on it keeps increasing. But what am I complaining about, it's only been going on for sixty-two years. I have to admit that's a lie. I enjoy telling lies. You see, when I lie I tell you it's a lie. That means it's not a lie, which is not true.

And I don't know about you, but I could do without all those new telephone-answering machines. I happen to prefer being face to face with whomever I'm talking to. I like to see how my stuff is going over. I've never been comfortable with a telephone, and that dates all the way back to that first call when Alexander Graham Bell said, "George, can you hear me?"

So you can imagine how I feel talking to an answering machine. And what frustrates me even more is waiting for that wise guy on the cassette to finish his monologue. Why does everyone with an answering machine think he has to do ten minutes? And if he's going to be so funny, let him hire writers like I did for mine.

The latest thing is these gadgets that talk to you. You can now be awakened by a talking alarm clock and then go into the bathroom and have your talking scale tell you that you're overweight. In the kitchen a talking toaster asks you how you prefer your toast, the coffeemaker asks you how strong you want the coffee, and the refrigerator informs you you're out of bread and coffee. The only one not talking to you is your wife. You bought all this stuff and she wanted a fur coat.

Gadgets have their place, but we've OD'd on them. We used to need big houses because we had big families. Now we need them for all the equipment we own. I'm not knocking these inventions. They save steps and they make life easier and more enjoyable, but they also break down. Sometimes two or three at a time. And that's real aggravation, because they have yet to come up with the invention we need the most: a repairman who will show up the day he said he would.

A few years ago I got one of those automatic garage door openers. It still works, only lately it's been opening my neighbor's garage instead of mine. But then his started opening mine instead of his. So Daniel, the male half of the couple who works for me, offered to take both the openers and have them fixed.

"That's silly," I said. "Why don't I just put my car in his garage and let him put his car in mine? We'll trade garages."

"You could do that," he said. And then as I was wondering why I have to think of everything, he added, "But it would be simpler to just trade openers."

Sometimes I think I should be working for him. Sometimes I think he shares that opinion. Well, it would never work out. I couldn't

With Daniel and Arlette. It's not easy to keep good help these days.

live on what I pay him. And I could never do for Daniel and Arlette the things they do for me. Somehow they manage to handle most of the household problems that come up. That spares me a lot of the daily aggravation most of you probably experience.

Not that there isn't plenty left for me. It's very annoying to have to hold my own martini glass. Those things are heavy, especially with an olive in it. And how about putting a cigar into my holder fifteen times a day? It takes both hands. I've got to put down my martini glass to do it. And what good is getting a cigar into your holder if you run out of matches? I tried to use a lighter, but my thumb was still sore from trying to open that peanut butter jar.

Look, I don't believe in aggravation. I don't let it keep me up nights. When I go to bed nothing bothers me. If it does, I tell her to leave.

For most people, dealing with aggravation doesn't seem to be that simple. Almost everyone I know in Hollywood has been to at least one psychiatrist. But that's becoming old hat. There are all sorts of new ways to go. Jogging is still "in," and memberships in health clubs have skyrocketed. Pumping iron, riding exercise bicycles that don't go anywhere, and jumping up and down to disco music are help-ing millions of people reduce the stress and tension in their lives, as well as the money in their wallets.

Then there's a thing called biofeedback. Don't ask me what that is. For all I know, biofeedback is what happens when your food repeats on you.

The other night I was watching one of those magazine shows on television, and they were demonstrating some other ways of escaping the aggravations in everyday life. One couple had built themselves a chamber in their garage for something called "primal screaming." You get into this big box, shut it tight and scream your lungs out until all the tension disappears or your neighbors ask you to move. This would do nothing for me. I take that back. It would probably hurt my vocal cords, and I'm a country singer.

Another group on the show was into some-thing called "Somati tanks." They're all the rage in Los Angeles. They're also called sen-sory deprivation tanks. I thought Somati tanks were something they used to hold fresh fish for Japanese food. You float in this dark tank filled with water at body temperature. The idea is to remove yourself from the out-side world and concentrate only on your inner self. The peace and quiet helps you relax and get in touch with yourself.

Being the adventurous soul that I am, I thought I'd try it. I filled my bathtub with lukewarm water, fixed myself a martini, lit a cigar, turned out the lights and got in. Then I had another martini, and then another. You know, I think Somati might really have something there.

I don't know if meditation is as big as it was a few years ago, but it still has lots of followers who practice it faithfully. Marsha Mason is one of the true believers. She says that meditation has changed her life, that it has given her spiritual strength and inner peace. As busy as she is with her career, she finds time for frequent trips to India to visit with her guru.

Which reminds me of the story about Mrs. Goldberg, who goes to her travel agent in Brooklyn and says she wants to fly to Nepal. He asks her if this is her first trip to Asia and she says it is. He tells her there are lots of other places there she would be better off seeing, but she insists on going to Nepal.

So she gets to Nepal, and right away she wants to go up the mountain where the guru is. They all tell her it's a tough trip up the mountain, but she doesn't care—that's where she wants to go. So they round up some donkeys, get her up the mountain, and she announces she wants to see the guru. They tell her this is not the guru's visiting hours; he's contemplating in privacy. She says she came all the way to see the guru and she wants to see the guru. She carries on so much they finally go and get the guru, and Mrs. Goldberg takes a look at him in his beard, robe and sandals, and says, "Sheldon, you look ridiculous. Put on a decent suit and come home already!"

I don't know why I'm suddenly so full of stories. I never tell other people's stories on the stage. I get my laughs the old-fashioned way, I *earn* them.

For those of you who believe in meditation, I didn't mean to offend you. I don't happen to believe in meditation, but I know something about it because a girl I went out with some time ago spent half the dinner talking about it. She told me she had been into it since it started in the sixties. I didn't have the heart to tell her meditation was actually a few thousand years old. I didn't want to give away my age.

She asked me if I had a mantra. I said no, but I had a cat. She explained that a mantra is something you hum when you're meditating, and she started humming. "Ommmmm-mmmmmmmmmmmm . . . Ommmmmmmmmm-mmmm . . . Ommmmmmmmmmmmm." It wasn't bad, but personally I'd rather listen to Julio Iglesias.

When we got back to my house she said if I got down on the floor she'd show me the lotus position and we'd do it together. It sounded exciting, but when we sat on the floor she explained this was meditation yoga style. She said I'd have to think of a word I could concentrate on, and she folded her legs like a pretzel and told me to do the same. I asked if she didn't think this was pretty silly. She said she didn't. And I said I didn't either, I thought it was stupid. That must have upset her, because before I could get up she was out the door and gone.

As long as I was on the floor I figured I might as well try it. Maybe there was something to this after all. So I folded my legs like a pretzel and tried to think of a word. After a half hour I tried to unfold my legs but I was stuck. Then the word came to me. It was "Help!" But nobody heard me—Daniel and Arlette were away for the weekend. So I dragged myself over to the telephone and called the fire department. They were just terrific. They rushed right over, smashed in the door, untangled my legs and the whole thing took only five minutes. The new door cost me $800.

Dr. Burns operating.

Thursday's Prescription

Dr. George Burns, H.S.
(HAPPINESS SPECIALIST)

DATE_____

NAME_____

ADDRESS_____

Thursday

Pay wife big compliment before bedtime.

If results indicate, repeat each night thereafter until out of compliments or strength.

GB

R̥

VI

A Hobby Can Be Fun (Especially If Your Wife Doesn't Find Out)

I'VE ALWAYS SUSPECTED that people who have hobbies were happier than people who didn't. A few days ago to find out if I was right, I took my own private poll. I stood on the corner of Wilshire and Rodeo Drive, stopped ten people passing by and asked them if they had a hobby. Seven told me to mind my own business, and the other three didn't speak English. I guess Dr. Gallup must use a different corner.

But I still say, if you have something that holds your interest, something that you can throw yourself into and get your mind off your work for a few hours a day, it has to be good for you.

There's a famous old story, about a theater manager who comes out just before the curtain and says, "There'll be no show tonight, our leading man just passed away." Some guy in the balcony hollers, "Give him an enema!" The manager says, "He's dead, how would that help?" The guy shouts back, "It wouldn't hurt!"

It's the same with a hobby. It can't hurt and it might be very helpful. If you live by yourself, a hobby can give you something to occupy your time. If you're married, a hobby can be something for you and your wife to share. If you're happily married, you might not need a hobby. And if you're dating a different girl every night, you have enough hobbies as it is.

I have a daily routine that I never deviate from. I may have mentioned this in a previous book. One of these days I'm going to have to sit down and read my books so I'll know what I've said before. There may be stuff I've repeated. And if it was worth repeating once, I can certainly repeat it again. Anyway, I get to my office every day at ten in the morning, work with my writers as hard as I can on whatever has to be done, and at twelve sharp, no matter where we are, even if I'm in the middle of a sentence, I drop everything and head for the Hillcrest Country Club. I have lunch there, and then from one until three I play bridge. This in my hobby and it's been going on for years.

Not everyone at my golf club plays bridge. Some play gin rummy, some play poker, some play pinochle, some play casino. One or two

76

even play golf.

I used to play golf. I took lessons, had expensive clubs, nice knickers, but it didn't work out. For one thing, nobody wanted to play with me. The problem was if I was playing well, I'd sing. That would annoy the other golfers. If I was playing badly, I'd sing even louder to keep my mind off my lousy game. So you see, I wasn't too popular to play with.

I played with Harpo Marx all the time, and I remember once when he parred the first hole, got a birdie on the second and parred the third. That was the best start he ever had. I didn't sing, I didn't smoke, I didn't breathe. I didn't want to do anything to upset him.

The next hole was a par 5 and his third shot went into a sand trap on top of a hill. And to keep out of his way I stayed at the bottom of the hill. He got all set for his next shot, then he stopped and looked down at me. He said, "Why are you standing down there?"

I said, "I didn't want to distract you."

"Well," he said, "that's exactly what you're doing. Come up here and just act natural."

So I went up there, but I was afraid even to look at him. Again he stopped his swing and said, "Why aren't you looking at me?"

So I looked at him. He swung and missed the ball completely. Then he came at me with his 9-iron and chased me into the clubhouse. When we got there we had coffee and cheese-cake, I sang him a song, he harmonized with me and that was the end of it.

Another time I was playing with Lou Clayton of Clayton, Jackson and Durante. He was a very good golfer, but on the second nine he shanked a 2-iron into the lake. It upset him so much that he picked up his big bag with all those beautiful clubs and threw them into the lake, too. I couldn't believe it. I said to him, "Lou, why do you play golf?" And he said, "It relaxes me."

I was never a good golfer. It aggravated me that I couldn't break a hundred, that I couldn't come home and tell Gracie I shot an eighty. So one day I came home and told Gracie I shot an eighty and I felt better. And then I found out I didn't have to play golf at all, I could play bridge and come home and say I shot an eighty.

That's when I gave up golf as a hobby and took up bridge. And for me it's been the perfect outlet. Every hand's a new challenge, and it takes complete concentration. You forget everything else. Sometimes I forget I'm playing bridge I concentrate so hard.

One day I was on my way to the game and I passed one of our former club presidents.

He said, "Hello, George," and I said, "Hello, kid." This annoyed him, and he said, "George, we've both been members of this club for over fifty years, and every time I see you I say, 'Hello, George,' and you say 'Hello, kid.' I'll bet you don't even know my name."

"Of course I do," I said. "I just don't know how to spell it."

He said, "S-C-H-I-F-F."

"Oh," I said, "so that's how you spell Schiff."

He said, "That's right, kid," and walked away.

Now I'm going to tell you about the fellows I play bridge with. You're not going to believe this so you better hold on to your book. I don't want you to fall down. It's quite a group. We're all about the same age, but some of the boys are hard of hearing and wear hearing aids. And one of them is very forgetful. He has that thing in his ear but keeps forgetting the battery. So I said to him, "Artie, a hearing aid without a battery isn't much of an aid." He said, "Thanks, George, and you look good, too."

One day we were playing and two of them forgot their hearing aids and the other one had a cold. I opened the first hand with a bid of one spade; the opponent to my left said a

*Thought you'd like to see the three old guys I
play with.*

heart; my partner said one diamond; and the fourth guy said a club. I said, "Goodbye, gentlemen, we'll play tomorrow." And Artie said, "Thanks, George, and you look good, too."

Another time I was playing with the same group. They were all in great shape; they had their batteries, their hearing aids, they had cleaned their glasses and nobody had a cold. They were really ready. And Artie was my partner. Our opponents had a sensational hand and bid seven no-trump. Artie was in the lead and he laid down the ace of spaces. I said, "Why the hell didn't you double?" He said, "I was afraid they would go into another suit." I said, "Thanks, Artie, and you look good, too."

Another tremendous hand I remember; this one was about eight or nine years ago when I was playing with three men who were much older than I was. One of the guys I was playing against opened with two spades, my partner passed, and his partner said four no-trump, asking for aces. The original bidder said five hearts, showing two aces. His partner had everything else, so he said, "Seven spades." Then very quietly I said, "Gentlemen, count your cards." There was silence for about a minute. The original bidder put a nitroglycerin pill under his tongue, and his partner said, "I'll take one, too." Then he very slowly counted his cards and said, "I've got thirteen." My partner said he had thirteen. The other opponent was shaking so I had to count his cards—he had thirteen. Then I counted mine, and said, "I've got thirteen, too, let's continue the game." And after the paramedics revived them, we did.

Incidentally, for those of you who don't understand bridge, I should tell you if you write to the publisher, you're not going to get your money back. But I'll make it up to you. Here's something you'll understand, it's a quickie. This ninety-year-old man was arrested and charged with rape. He was so flattered he pleaded guilty. That's the end of the joke.

Now back to hobbies. Wait—one more bridge story. Chico Marx, who loved to gamble, went into a bridge club in San Francisco, and except for four fellows playing bridge the place was empty. It was a game where you couldn't cut in unless one of the players quit. So Chico took one of them aside and whispered, "You're being cheated. That guy in the blue suit, when he holds his cigarette on the left side of his mouth that means he's got clubs. When he puts the cigarette in the center of his mouth that means he's got diamonds. If it's on the right side, he's got hearts, and when he doesn't put the cigarette in his mouth at all that means spades." The man thanked Chico profusely, quit the game, Chico took his place, lost $1200 and had a great afternoon.

Back to hobbies. To be a good hobby it should hold your interest. And if you get a sense of satisfaction from it, so much the better. Painting, sculpting, carving, furniture making, glass blowing—they all make great hobbies. The more you do them the better you get, and the better you get the more pleasure they give you.

Photography also makes an excellent hobby. It takes knowledge, patience and a sense of what makes an interesting composition. It also takes a camera. I'm not knocking photographers, but I've always felt that if I snapped a thousand pictures of a hummingbird, I too would end up with one that everybody would rave about. I must say photography is not for me. If I'm going into a dark room for three hours to see what develops, it certainly won't be with a lot of hummingbirds.

But that's me. Photography enthusiasts love their hobby. Some of them are in dark rooms so much they grow fungus. And there's nothing they won't do to get a good picture. I was in the men's room of the Beverly-Wilshire Hotel recently, doing what you do in men's rooms, when all of a sudden there was a flash. And there is this guy with a Polaroid taking my picture. I was very upset. I made him do it again—I wasn't smiling.

Cooking has become a big hobby lately. A lot of men are into cooking. In fact, some of the best cooks I know are men. Also some of the worst. Those are the ones I get invitations from. They love to have me over, and they always serve something they've had simmering for about three days, which means every time they pass the pot they throw something else in. Male cooks seem to pride themselves on not using recipe books. With them it's instinct. They cook by the seat of their pants, and usually that's what it tastes like. And when they serve it to you they announce this is their own concoction and don't ask how they made it because they're not telling. You're looking for a place to hide it and they're worried about someone stealing their secret. Look, it's their hobby. If they enjoy cooking, they should cook, but they should eat it, too. Leave me out of it.

It's nice to have a hobby you're enthused about, but you can get carried away. People with those elaborate model train sets have this tendency. I have a neighbor who is a real nut. We call him Engineer Bill. He's got more track in his house than Union Pacific. And he's adding to it. The set occupies three rooms, with a fortune in bridges, warehouses, little villages and tunnels for the trains to run through. Last year he re-created the entire state of Vermont in miniature, including two drunks passed out behind a bowling alley in Montpelier.

That train set is his life. Nothing else matters. He's always playing with his trains. And while he's playing with his trains, his wife is out playing with his friends. He has his hobby and she's got hers.

The most important thing about a hobby is that it be something you do because you want to, not because you have to. For years my cousin Louie was one of the best dress cutters in New York City. But the pressures of work were giving him ulcers, insomnia and heart palpitations. Everyone kept telling him he needed a hobby. So he decided to start collecting those painted wooden horses from amusement park carousels. I would have picked something more exciting, like antique door knockers. But for Louie it worked. Soon he not only felt great but he found that he was making good money trading his horses with other collectors. He did so well that he quit his job so he could pursue his hobby full time. But now the hobby became a business, and within a year his ulcers were so bad that he needed a hobby again. You guessed it—cutting dresses.

If you avoid Louie's mistake, you could do worse than have a hobby that involved collecting things. There is almost no limit to your choice. You can collect anything from butterflies to shrunken heads. And I've never understood why, but with a lot of collections the less the things are worth, the more valuable the collection is: beat-up bottle tops, old baseball cards, illegible writing on torn scraps of parchment, out-of-date stamps—a 2-cent stamp from the year 1721 is worth more than my house in Beverly Hills. I know someone who had that stamp. He's now divorced. He got the kids, the house and the car; she got the stamp. The last I heard he was contesting.

Another fellow I know collects guns. He's got pistols and rifles from all over the world from the time they were invented down to the present day. He has them stacked on every shelf and in every closet. About three months ago he and his wife were awakened by a burglar robbing their house. He told me later the thief got away with all his wife's jewelry.

"With all those guns," I asked, "why didn't you stop him?"

"Are you crazy?" he said. "I wouldn't touch those guns. They're too valuable."

I said, "You're lucky he didn't take your wife," and he said, "That's your opinion."

None of this should discourage you from starting some kind of a collection. However, I do have several warnings. First, don't collect big-game animals like lions or tigers if you live in an apartment, especially if the elevator operator doesn't have a sense of humor.

Second, make sure you don't go around collecting stuff that belongs to someone else, or you'll have ten years to think of a new hobby, that is if you get a kind judge.

Third, and most important of all, the worst mistake you can possibly make is to ———

I'm sorry, it's twelve o'clock.

The Nine Happiest Animals

1. **THE HORSE**
    He sleeps standing up and doesn't know what it is to spend the night in a crummy hotel.

2. **THE OSTRICH**
    He can be the happiest of all, but when he takes his head out of that sand he's in trouble like the rest of us.

3. **THE RABBIT**
    Because he's always . . . (censored)

4. **THE MINK**
    (Same as above)

5. **THE ELEPHANT**
    He's been to just about every country and he has yet to lose his trunk.

6. **THE MOOSE**
    No matter what, he'll always have a place to hang his hat.

7. **THE HIPPOPOTAMUS**
    You'd be happy, too, if you could weigh

four thousand pounds and not have to go on a diet.

8.   THE PIGEON
Because it's not easy for us to do to him what he can do to us. (It's a good thing a hippopotamus can't fly.)

9.   THE PENGUIN
He must be having fun, he's always dressed like he's ready to have dinner at Chasen's.

I don't know why I have to stick to 9, I'm going to do 10—I might even do 11 or 12. This is 10:

10.   THE GNU
No matter how old he is he always looks gnu.

It sounded good when I thought of it, but on paper it's nothing. From now on I'm sticking to 9.

VII

Getting There Is Half the Fun (But It's the Other Half That Keeps Me Home)

THE OLDER I get the more I realize there are some things in this world I'll never understand. One is how you can get to be my age and have so many things you don't understand. Another is why so many people are happiest when they are anyplace but home.

A man pays three million for a house in Bel Air or Beverly Hills, his wife lays out $500,000 to redecorate it exactly to their taste, they throw in another $100,000 redoing the pool and the landscaping and putting in a lighted tennis court, and after all that they move in and two weeks later they've locked it up and are off to enjoy the back alleys of Tangiers or the sights, sounds and smells of the lower Ganges.

What's amazing is that they're not the exception. They have company at every level of income; enough to make the travel business a billion-dollar industry. For some, getting away means the two weeks of the year that make the other fifty bearable. Others only come home long enough to pick up the mail, holler at the kids, get some clean underwear, feed the dog and leave again.

Everyone is someplace else. If you were planning to go to Tokyo to see the Japanese, forget it. They're all over here snapping pictures of Marineland. The Germans are in Spain; the Spaniards are in North Africa; the North Africans are in France; the French are in Italy; the Italians are in Arabia; and the Arabs are everywhere. So are the Americans. If you want to see all your friends, go to London, Paris and Rome. If you want to meet interesting, exotic-looking foreigners, stay home.

I've seen lots of tourists in my time, and there are as many different kinds as there are countries. Some want everything done for them. They travel with groups on charters or organized tours where every detail is taken care of. When they get home they can't always tell you where they've been, but they'll do two hours on how smoothly things went.

Others are just the opposite. They wouldn't think of going with a group. And they don't even use travel agents, they do it themselves. I know a couple like that. Every time they go anywhere they spend months looking at maps, doing research, making up itineraries and writing away for reservations. They love planning their trip, and they love talking about it when they get back. The only thing they don't love is the trip itself. That they could do without.

Some people are only happy in out-of-the-way places, staying among the natives and living like they do. Others can be in France, India, Egypt or Tibet, it's all the same to them, because they're always in an American hotel where they eat only American food and stay in their room all day watching "I Love Lucy" reruns and sending local picture postcards to everyone they ever knew.

Then there are the shoppers. They don't go to see a country, they go to buy it. Whatever this year's bargains are is where you'll find them. One woman I know spent $10,000 dragging her husband all the way to Italy just to buy a pair of Italian alligator boots. They didn't tell her the alligator was from Florida. It was caught in a swamp about fifteen miles from their condominium in Fort Lauderdale.

And how about those happy travelers who only want to know three things about their trips: Where do we eat? What do we eat? and When do we eat? This is quite a large group, and they're getting larger by the meal. When they check into a hotel they don't want to see brochures on points of interest, they go right for the room-service menu. And they eat their way from country to country.

The other day I overheard two Jewish ladies in a restaurant in Beverly Hills. One had just returned from Paris and the other was asking about her trip. This was the conversation:

"So you liked the Champs?"

"Fantastic. Best crepes I ever had."

"And you got to the Eiffel?"

"Wouldn't have missed it. But the portions at the bottom don't compare to what they give you halfway up."

"And how about that Notre Dame!"

"They got a restaurant there?"

At least she enjoys herself. Some tourists complain from the minute they leave to the minute they get back: the bed's too hard, the bed's too soft, the room's filthy, the bus is too hot, the guide's rude, the château's a bore, the Riviera's a ripoff. If you give them the Seven Wonders of the World, they might be satisfied.

That's another thing I don't understand. What makes the Seven Wonders so wonderful, and who decided on them? I'm not putting down the Taj Mahal or the Great Wall of China, but when it comes to traveling these are some wonders I'd like to see:

A cabdriver who understands English, especially in America.

A place in the world where you can't get a Big Mac and a Coke.

A headwaiter who hides his scorn when you order the house wine.

A cruise ship that advertises "no gratuities" where you can actually skip the tip without running the risk of being thrown overboard.

And what about an airport, train station or bus terminal where you can understand the person announcing the departures and arrivals? That would really be a wonder of the world!

If you're getting the idea that travel is not my long suit, you're right. And yet I can understand why so many people can't wait to get away. For them it's an escape from the pressures of their daily life. I've never had that problem. I've always been able to turn it on and turn it off, although lately it seems to turn off easier than it turns on. And sometimes I don't have to turn it off, it turns off by itself.

The truth is I'm not a sightseer. I don't applaud anything that can't applaud back. And I'm not the kind to lie on a beach in the sun waiting for my skin to shrivel up. It does enough of that while I'm moving around.

I must say if I were the beach type and a year or two younger, I might give the Club Med a try. They have locations all over—the South Pacific, Mexico, the Caribbean—and their ads make it look very inviting. Lots of great-looking male and female bodies in lots of tan skin. And what activities! Tennis, golf, volleyball, sailing, scuba diving, surfing, dancing, drinking, and I think I left something out. Oh yes—investment counseling. I knew there was something I could do.

Actually, the only kind of travel I really enjoy is when it's a working trip. That gives it a purpose. When Gracie and I were in vaudeville we went all over the country to do our act. And when we traveled to England it wasn't to go through churches and museums, it was to play the Palladium or do a Command Performance for the Royal Family.

In 1982, years after I started working alone, they asked me to appear at the Royal Gala of the Barbican Centre in London. Prince

Charles and Lady Diana were to attend. When I arrived in England the newspaper reporters met me, and one of them asked what I thought of Lady Di. I said, "She's a little too old for me." Not the biggest joke in the world, but it made all the papers.

After the show at the Centre all the performers stood in line to meet the Royal Couple. When they got to me, Lady Di said, "I understand I'm too old for you."

I said, "No, ma'am," and Prince Charles said, "And she's not too old for me, either." I had a funnier line than "No, ma'am" for Lady Di, but I don't go around topping royalty. I love playing England.

It reminds me of another time I appeared for the Royal Family. This event took place at the Palladium for one of Princess Margaret's favorite charities. After the show they took me up to the Royal Box to meet Princess Margaret. Well, this charming lady was sitting there, and I said to her, "Your Highness, I'd bow, but if I got down I wouldn't be able to get up again." She said, "Mr. Burns, I'm not Princess Margaret, I'm the lady-in-waiting."

Just then the Princess came in, and after we were introduced, I said, "Your Highness, I just told a funny joke and you missed it." She said she was sorry, and she was also sorry she

The QE II. *That's me in the back waving.*

missed some of the lyrics of my last song. I said, "Would you like to hear it again?" and she said, "No, once is enough."

I figured it was time to leave, but as I started to go the attendant stopped me. "No, no," he whispered, "the Princess leaves first." I sat down, and after the Princess left I got up and he stopped me again and whispered, "The lady-in-waiting goes next." So I just sat there—I was afraid to move. Finally the usher came in and said, "Mr. Burns, everybody has gone, we're ready to close the theater." So I got up to leave, and he said, "No, I go first." I said, "Oh, you do?" "Yes," he said, "and don't forget to lock up on your way out."

Just a few months ago I had a most enjoyable working vacation when I was invited to perform on the *Queen Elizabeth II*. The last time I entertained on a ship was the *Leviathan* in 1926. They must have liked me because here it was fifty-eight years later and I was back entertaining on a ship again.

Irving Fein, my manager, accepted their offer. We flew to Hong Kong, spent a few days there, boarded the ship and went on to Bangkok and Singapore. In our party besides Irving and his wife, Marion, were my piano player, Morty Jacobs, and his wife, Madeline, and Cathy Carr, the lovely, lively young lady from Dallas who came into my life four years ago and makes me feel like I'm eighty again.

We all had a great time. First of all, the *QE II* is not a ship, it's a floating city. There's a shopping mall selling items from all over the world, a movie theater, a post office and a country club with two swimming pools and a nine-hole golf course. It's so big they should have bus service just to get around the decks.

They've got every activity imaginable, but you can't do any of it because they're serving food every twenty minutes. Irving brought along his jogging suit. He told me he was going to jog around the deck three times a day. The only jogging I saw him do was around the buffet table to make sure he didn't miss anything. He'll deny that, but all I know is he bought a suit in Hong Kong, and when we got to Bangkok five days later he couldn't get into it.

Cathy doesn't eat, she shops. I couldn't get her out of that mall. And Hong Kong never had it so good. She had two staterooms, one for her and one for all the stuff she bought. She bought so many things in Hong Kong she had to sell it all in Bangkok to make room for what she intended to buy in Singapore.

Cathy doesn't buy one of anything, or five of anything. She shops like she's a buyer for

Cathy and I in Bangkok. I think she just bought the building in back of us.

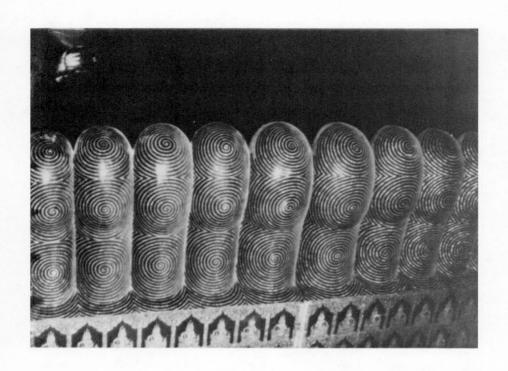

The toes of the Reclining Buddha. I told you photography wasn't my hobby.

Bloomingdale's. She came out of one shop in Hong Kong with four dozen handkerchiefs for me. I said, "This is it? This is all the handkerchiefs I get?"

"They're not for now," she explained. "They're for your birthdays. You get a dozen when you're eighty-nine, another when you're ninety, another when you're ninety-one and the fourth dozen when you're ninety-two."

I said, "Does this mean you're through with me when I'm ninety-three?"

"Oh no," she said. "When you're ninety-three we'll come back and buy more handkerchiefs."

She bought everything: silver place settings, jewelry, clothes, China (not the country, the plates). In Bangkok we went to see the famous Reclining Buddha. It's ninety feet long and made of gold. "George, isn't that magnificent," she whispered. "What do you think that Buddha weighs?"

I said, "Forget it, Cathy, it's not for sale."

All through the trip Cathy had been studying her Thai language book so she'd be ready when we got to Bangkok. The first store we went into there had everything. She saw some silver candlesticks she liked, so she took out her little book and tried to talk to the clerk about them. After a few minutes he gave up and walked away. I said, "Cathy, they all speak English."

"George," she said, "I'm having fun, let me enjoy myself. When in Rome do as the Romans do."

"They speak English, too," I said.

But she wanted to do it her way, and she went through the entire thing again with another clerk. He kept nodding, and she said, "You understand, don't you?"

"Oh yes," he said, "except for one thing. What are you going to do with a live monkey?" That's when Cathy gave me the book.

But that wasn't the end of it. She had just decided on a pair of candlesticks when Irving came over. Now Irving Fein is not my manager for nothing. He said to Cathy. "Let me handle this, I'll get you a better price." He said it to her in English and she understood. So he asked the clerk how much the candlesticks were in American money, and the clerk said, "Thirty dollars apiece."

Irving said, "How much for cash?"

"Thirty dollars apiece."

"How much for four candlesticks?"

"Thirty dollars apiece."

Irving said, "Down the street they're selling the same candlesticks for twenty dollars apiece."

With that rickshaw driver in Singapore.

I guess he doesn't realize he's being pedaled by a man who performed for the Queen.

The clerk said, "Why didn't you buy them there?"

"They were out of them," Irving replied.

The clerk said, "If I was out of them, I'd give them to you for fifteen dollars apiece."

"I like you," Irving said, "but thirty dollars is a lot for a candlestick."

And the clerk said, "I like you, too. I'll tell you what. If you buy them for thirty, I'll throw in the live monkey." Irving looked at me, and I said, "I'll explain it to you later."

Well, I don't know how he did it, but Irving ended up getting the candlesticks for $20 apiece. And to show you what a businessman he is, he went down the street and sold them to the guy who didn't have them for $35 apiece. But it turned out to be a losing proposition. With all that maneuvering we missed the last tender back to the ship, and hiring another boat to get us out there cost us three times what Irving made on the candlesticks.

A few days later we were in Singapore, where we stayed three nights at the Pavilion Intercontinental, one of their newest and finest hotels. I had been walking around and wanted to get back to the hotel, so I got on one of those bicycle rickshaws they have there. The native driver had pedaled me a few blocks when who did we run into but Irving.

He asked the driver how much he was charging me, and when the driver told him, Irving said, "That's ridiculous!" But rather than have him go through that whole thing again I got on the bicycle, put the driver in the passenger compartment and pedaled us to my hotel.

Singapore was as fascinating in its own way as Hong Kong and Bangkok. And what amazed us was that in all of these places wherever I went the natives would wave or point at me and call my name. They knew me from my movies and TV shows. Outside the Pavilion Intercontinental a man asked me to autograph a book he had that was written in Japanese. I looked at it, and it was my last book, *How to Live to Be 100—Or More*. I must be a better author than I thought—I didn't know I could write in Japanese. I autographed it, gave it back to him, he bowed three times and left. I don't know why he was taking bows. I wrote a book in Japanese, I should be taking the bows.

I also found the people on board ship to be very fascinating. And very rich. To take an eighty-day trip around the world on the *QE II* with the best accommodations costs a quarter of a million dollars. One woman told me this was her twentieth trip. I had tea with her in the lounge one day, and she asked me where the bathroom was. Imagine that—her twentieth trip and she still didn't know. I guess the rich really are different.

Another lady that Cathy and I had coffee with had so much jewelry on she could hardly move. She had rings on every finger, and the jewels were so big she couldn't close her hands. I can't close my hands, but it's arthritis. I go to a doctor; she goes to Tiffany's. I really haven't got arthritis, but if I can get a laugh, I'll even admit to an ingrown toenail.

Between performing and shopping, the sightseeing and having Cathy read me the daily papers in Thai, the two weeks went by like two days. I'm glad I went, but that takes care of the traveling for a while. That trip will last me until I'm ninety-three and need more handkerchiefs.

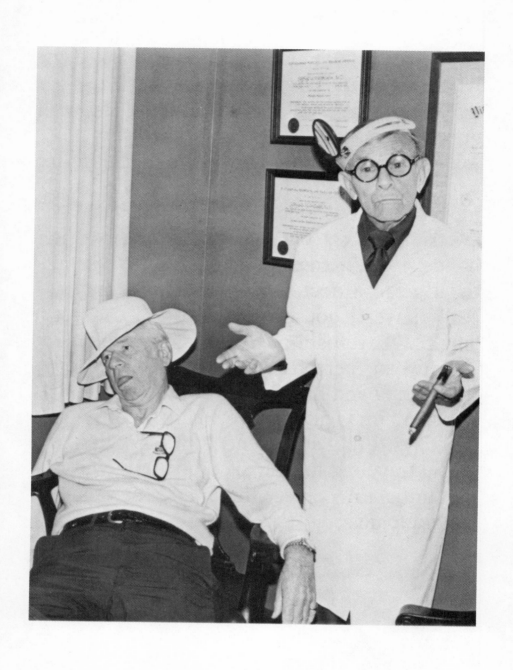

You win a few, you lose a few.

Friday's Prescription

Dr. George Burns, H.S.
(HAPPINESS SPECIALIST)

DATE_____

NAME_____

ADDRESS_____

Friday

For that all around good feeling--
1) Put neighbor's paper on porch.
2) Switch off headlights on
    unattended car.
3) Help little old lady across street.

Possible side effects

Being charged with :
1) Trespassing.
2) Car theft.
3) Attempted assault.

℞

GB

More Definitions of Happiness

Happiness is:

Getting a driver's license photo that doesn't look like you've passed away.

Being audited by the IRS and discovering that they owe *you* money.

Your mother-in-law developing an untreatable allergy to something in your house.

Your mistress coming down with morning sickness and finding out it's only from some bad sausage she ate.

VIII

You Can't Say I Didn't Try

WHEN YOU READ a book you see what's there on the page and you judge it accordingly. You have no way of knowing what went on behind the scenes, why certain things were put in and others left out, and that the writer may not always have the last word.

As an example of what we authors have to contend with, you might be interested in a phone conversation that took place a while back. I had just come up with a brilliant idea for getting forty or fifty hilarious pages for this book. In fact, when it came to me I got so excited I jumped up and did the Charleston. And I immediately put in a long-distance call to my publisher, Phyllis Grann. Since I happened to tape the whole thing, we don't even have to trust my memory. Here is our conversation, word for word:

Sound: Phone ringing . . . receiver up

PHYLLIS: Hello. Phyllis Grann here.
GEORGE: Phyllis . . . this is George Burns.

PHYLLIS: George! I've been thinking about you. How are you doing?

GEORGE: Great. Got a minute?

PHYLLIS: For you, anything.

GEORGE: I'll remember that. But I called about the book.

PHYLLIS: Oh good, you're done!

GEORGE: No, but it's going great, just great.

PHYLLIS: How far are you?

GEORGE: I'm starting the second chapter.

PHYLLIS: . . . I think we've got a bad connection. It sounded like you said you're starting the second chapter.

GEORGE: That's what I said.

PHYLLIS: I don't believe this. Two months and you're just starting the second chapter?

GEORGE: But I've got all my thoughts for it.

PHYLLIS: Congratulations. What happened to the George Burns who writes like he talks?

GEORGE: He's talking slower these days.

PHYLLIS: This is serious. You promised I'd have it in time to get it out for Christmas. Can't we do something to speed things up?

GEORGE: That's exactly why I called. You remember *How to Live to Be 100— Or More?*

PHYLLIS: Of course. You knocked that out for me in six weeks.

GEORGE: Seven. But you know, it just occurred to me, all those great chapters—the one on exercises, the one on diet, the positive attitude, the one about relatives—they would have worked in this book, too.

PHYLLIS: So what?

GEORGE: So I'll change it from longevity to happiness. A few words here, a few words there, and we got ourselves some fresh, funny stuff, right?

PHYLLIS: What are you talking about?

GEORGE: I'm talking about fifty pages. And if we look, I bet we can find another couple of chapters. That'll give us eighty pages and you'll have your book out by the Fourth of July.

PHYLLIS: You can't be serious.

GEORGE: This is long distance—I'm serious.

PHYLLIS: But, George, you can't just take from another book.

GEORGE: Why not? It's not Art Buchwald's book I'm taking from, it's mine. What am I gonna do, sue myself?

PHYLLIS: What about the person who bought the first book? Now he buys this one and suddenly he finds he's reading the same material all over again.

GEORGE: First of all, he must have liked the material in the first one or he wouldn't be buying the second one, so maybe he won't mind reading the same material over again. And how come you're so worried about him? What about the guy who just buys the second book and never bought the first one? Is it fair for me to deprive him of all that good stuff?

PHYLLIS: George, if it were all right to do what you are suggesting, everybody would be writing books.

GEORGE: Everybody is.

PHYLLIS: Why are we arguing? Take my word, George, it's never been done in the history of publishing.

GEORGE: Good, we'll have a first.

PHYLLIS: George, listen carefully. Are you listening?

GEORGE: I'm listening.

Sound: Click of phone being hung up

That ended that. I don't know why I even

bothered calling her. She wasn't all that much help on the difference between a foreword and a preface.

Saturday's Prescription

DR. GEORGE BURNS, H.S.
(HAPPINESS SPECIALIST)

DATE_____

NAME_____

ADDRESS_____

Saturday

Repeat 3 times a day :

"Happiness is within me.
Material things mean nothing."

When convinced, give all your
money to charity.

But not before you pay
my bill.

GB   ℞

The doctor resting between patients.

Nine Ways to Make Your Wife Happy

1. When you get home from work don't tell her about your problems at the office, let her talk about her problems. And if you're one of her problems, don't listen.

2. Surprise her with a sweater two sizes too small. She'll be flattered, she'll love you for it, and since she can't wear it, give it back to your secretary.

3. When you're with her watching a Bo Derek movie, say, "Come on, sweetheart, let's get out of here. I don't know what they see in her."

4. Instead of reading the newspaper at the kitchen table, try talking to your wife. You might learn a few things, like your kids have grown up and moved out.

5. Remember those important dates: her birthday, Valentine's Day, your anniversary, your first date together, your first trip together, and above all what happened the day you forgot one of those days you were supposed to remember.

6. Praise her in public. Let her hear you telling others how much you depend on her judgment and value her intelligence. What you say behind her back is up to you.

7. Call her from the office three or four times a day to chat. Take her to a long lunch once or twice a week. And never bring your work home with you. You might miss a promotion or lose your job, but your wife will be happy.

8. Take her on a second honeymoon. And this time it won't matter if she hides in the bathroom.

9. If all of the above have failed and you still want to make her happy, try leaving her.

(NOTE: If she's working, or if she's working and you aren't, Nos. 1 and 7 may not apply. If neither of you is working, you shouldn't be reading this book, you should be out looking for a job.)

Nine Ways to Make Your Girlfriend Happy

Don't worry about it. Your girlfriend should make *you* happy. If she doesn't, you might as well be with your wife.

IX

Happiness Is Offering a Helping Hand
(And Maybe the Rest of Your Body, Too)

*I*F YOU WERE to go around asking people what would make them happier, you'd get answers like a new car, a bigger house, a raise in pay, winning a lottery, a face-lift, more kids, less kids, a new restaurant to go to—probably not one in a hundred would say a chance to help people. And yet that may bring the most happiness of all.

I don't know Dr. Jonas Salk, but after what he's done for us with his polio vaccine, if he isn't happy, he should have that brilliant head of his examined. Of course, not all of us can do what he did. I know I can't do what he did; he beat me to it.

But the point is, it doesn't have to be anything that extraordinary. It can be working for a worthy cause, performing a needed service, or just doing something that helps another person.

I don't think there is any other profession that is as generous and unselfish as mine. Performers can count on each other for whatever is needed, be it money, advice or just moral support. If at the last minute some young actor gets sick and can't play a date, they can always count on me to take his place.

When it comes to doing "freebies" on telethons and benefits, the same people are called upon over and over again, and rarely do they fail to respond. Jan Murray does a great routine about his agent who doesn't get him paying jobs anymore, or even benefits. Now it's just parties. And even that's a struggle. If the agent doesn't answer his call, that means the Marvin Davis party fell through.

In all honesty I must say most of the comedians I hang around with would be insulted if you invited them to your party and didn't ask them to get up and perform. Everyone gets up and performs. And it's always the same little game; they're asked by the host to get up and do something for the group, and invariably they'll say, "What? Again I gotta work for my supper? Forget it!" And then, with the host trying to pull him to the center of the room, "No, no! Come on, gimme a break! I got a sore throat. Please, not this time, ask Danny Thomas." And if the host lets go of his arm and asks Danny Thomas, that comedian will never set foot in that house again.

And it's important who comes off best. If Red Buttons is a bigger hit than Buddy Hackett, Buddy's evening is ruined. If it happens two parties in a row, Buddy could go looking for new writers. So even though everyone tries to make it look as if their routine just came to them, they work very hard preparing their party material. The trouble is the same comedians keep popping up at all the parties, and there are so many parties that there isn't always time to prepare new stuff, so you keep hearing the same old ad-lib bits over and over. It got so I knew Jack Carter's stuff better than my own. One night I forgot myself and was halfway through his routine before he came out of the bathroom and did what he had just done. It ruined my finish; I couldn't do my sand dance.

We all kid each other. That's the business. But we help each other, too. And I don't think there's one of us who wouldn't do what he could to give a newcomer a boost. I know it makes me feel good that I was able to help some very big talents get their careers going. Let me tell you about one of them.

When I was just starting to work alone I was looking for some talent to put together a show. I heard a record called "Splish Splash" by some kid named Bobby Darin, so I sent for him. Into my office came this middle-aged-looking man, about six feet two and weighing about 280 pounds. This was not what I expected. I said, " 'Splish Splash'— you must have made a bigger splash than the record."

He said, "I'm not Bobby Darin, I'm his manager." Then he brought Bobby in, and I liked him the minute I saw him. Two weeks later he was part of my show in Lake Tahoe. As soon as Bobby walked on the stage the audience fell in love with him. After Tahoe I took him to Vegas with me, Bobby's recording of "Mack the Knife" came out and was a big hit, and things began happening fast for him. We got to be very close; he looked up to me like a father.

One night I heard that he had won $1500 at the crap table, so I went into his dressing room and said, "Bobby, what are you going to do with all the money?"

He said, "I'm on a roll, I'm going to win more."

"Give me thirteen hundred of it, and you gamble with the other two hundred," I said. "That's enough for you to lose. At the end of the date I'll give you back the thirteen hundred."

He said, "No, Mr. Burns. I'm not a kid—

Elvis Presley and Bobby Darin. I don't think they even knew I was there.

I'm twenty-two years old. I know what I'm doing."

Sure enough, he went back to the crap table and lost it all, plus another two hundred. When I heard about it I got very angry. I walked into his dressing room and said, "You ought to be ashamed of yourself, losing seventeen hundred dollars! That's a lot of money for a kid like you to lose!" Then I slapped him and walked out. I had to; if he had hit me back he would have killed me.

Ordinarily, before Bobby came on I gave him a very glowing introduction, but not that night. I just said, "Ladies and gentlemen, here he is, Bobby Darin," and started to walk off. Bobby ran out and grabbed me. He was very upset. "Mr. Burns," he said, "unless you give me that other introduction I won't be able to do my act!"

I said, "We'll let the audience decide." I told them the whole story and ended with, "Do you think a kid like this deserves a good introduction?" They all shouted "Yeah!" So I gave him the good introduction, Bobby and I hugged and he was a riot. He must have learned his lesson, because that night he stayed away from the crap table. I know; I was there. I lost $500.

Bobby Darin was a tremendous talent and

he came out on the stage with all the confidence in the world. Some people thought he was a brash, cocky kid. And in some ways he was. When he was twenty-two he told the press that at twenty-five he was going to be a living legend. The kid gave himself three years. I'm eighty-eight, and if I'm going to be a living legend by ninety-one, I better get busy.

Underneath all that bravado Bobby Darin was a very caring, sensitive person. I remember when Robert Kennedy was assassinated, Bobby was just shattered. Kennedy was his idol. It changed his whole attitude toward life. He gave up rock 'n' roll to sing meaningful folk songs. Instead of a big orchestra he started using a four-piece combo. He stopped wearing his toupee, grew a beard and instead of that sharp tuxedo he came out wearing faded old blue jeans and a sweatshirt. He was playing nothing but small clubs and coffee houses.

One night I went to see him at the Troubadour, a little coffee house in West Hollywood. I couldn't get over it. After the show I went backstage to see him. I said, "Bobby, what are you doing? This isn't you. Get rid of that beard and those clothes. Get back into your tuxedo. And put on your toupee. If you

Ann-Margret—1960.

Ann-Margret—1983.

haven't got one, I'll loan you one. You want to do something for Bobby Kennedy, do your old act, make a lot of money again and give half of it to the Kennedy Foundation." That's exactly what he did, and he was as big a smash as ever.

Bobby was like a son to me, and I still miss him.

Now I'd like to do a few minutes on Ann-Margret. When I first saw her she was only nineteen years old and she had just arrived from Chicago, where she had been attending Northwestern University. She came into my office with her piano player and said, "Mr. Burns, I'd like to sing for you."

I said, "Why for me?"

"Well," she said, "I heard what you did for Bobby Darin, and I thought you might do the same for me."

I asked her if she could sing like Bobby Darin, and she said, "I don't know whether I sing as good as Bobby Darin, but I certainly move better than he does." She should have said, "I don't know whether I sing as *well* as Bobby Darin," but I didn't notice at the time. Now that I'm an author I'm aware of those things.

Anyway, there was a piano in the property room, so we all went back there. The place was covered with dust; it looked awful. But I wanted to hear her, so I said, "Okay, kid let me hear you sing a song."

And she did. And she was right, she did move better than Bobby Darin. By the time she got to the second chorus she had dusted every piece of furniture in the place. Then she threw in a couple of little wiggles that even cleaned the ashtrays.

I put her in my stage show, took her to Vegas and she was just terrific. Six months later I sent for her and said, "Annie, how about playing Las Vegas again?"

She said, "Oh, I'd love to. Let me hear you sing a song." I sang a song, and she took me.

I always enjoyed working with Ann-Margret. One time we were playing Vegas over the holidays, and on opening night she came off the stage and started to cry. I said, "Annie, why are you crying? The audience loved you." She said it was Christmas Eve and she missed her mother. So I told her to go into my dressing room and phone her mother and charge it to me. Then I went out on the stage to entertain. An hour later I went back to my dressing room and she was still on the phone. I sat there and waited until she was finished, then I said, "Annie, you're not crying anymore. Your mother was glad to hear from you, huh?"

She said, "Oh yes, Mr. Burns. We had a wonderful conversation."

I asked her why she didn't invite her mother to Las Vegas, and she told me she couldn't, her mother lived in Sweden. Then I started to cry.

With all that talent and beauty nothing could have kept Ann-Margret from being the big star she's become. But the fact is I did give Annie her first important platform, and, knowing that, I still get a good feeling every time I look at her. Who am I kidding? I'd get a good feeling looking at Ann-Margret if I'd never done anything for her. That kid can dust my furniture anytime.

You won't believe it, but another kid I helped was Frank Sinatra. He was in his early twenties at the time, and he had just left Tommy Dorsey. I was looking for a singer for the Burns & Allen radio show, and I was offered Sinatra for $250 a week. I was about to sign him when I learned I could get an act called The Three Smoothies for the same money. Well, I wasn't born yesterday—if I could get three people for the same money, what would I want with that skinny kid? So I took The Smoothies. Frank has never forgotten that.

Every Christmas I get a gift from him with a note thanking me for not doing for his career what I did for The Smoothies.

I'd like to tell you about some of the other stars that I helped, but I can't continue. I just remembered I'm invited to Steve Allen's house. He's giving a party tonight and I have to rehearse my ad-libs.

He still can't get over what I did for him.

Sunday's Prescription

DR. GEORGE BURNS, H.S.
(HAPPINESS SPECIALIST)

DATE_____

NAME_____

ADDRESS_____

Sunday

If previous prescriptions haven't made you happy, get a second opinion.

If they have made you happy, get one anyway.

GB

Note: If you are getting a second opinion, don't forget Dr. Burns has two offices.

℞

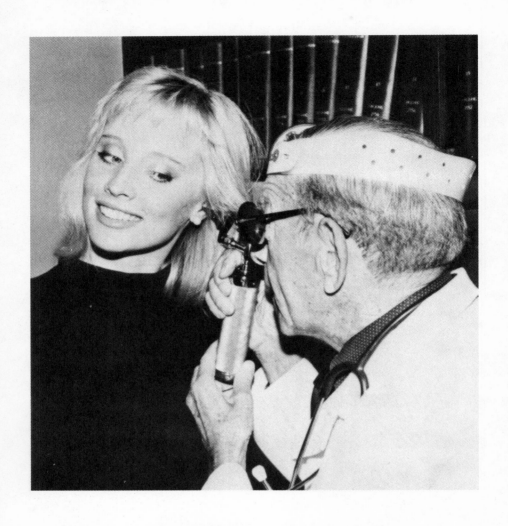

The doctor doing a little research.

X

Work Only Works If the Work You
Work at Isn't Work
(I Get Paid by the Word, so I Threw in Two More "Works")

*I*F YOU WERE to ask me to name one thing above all others that makes for happiness, I would say without fear of contradiction that it's enjoying your work. Wait—why should I fear contradiction? I fear tough audiences, drafty dressing rooms, makeup that streaks, but not contradiction. Everybody gets contradicted. Maybe not as often as I do, but it's nothing to fear. It's nothing to brag about either.

Let me put it this way. You can't be happy if you don't enjoy your work. Actually, that's not true in all cases. There are people who don't have any work to enjoy, who are retired or rich enough to get along without it, and who are still happy. They enjoy not having a job to go to or any kind of steady work. I don't understand them, but I know they're out there. Just like I know there are people who enjoy sitting on flagpoles, or tearing a telephone book in half, or swimming in Lake Michigan in twenty-below weather.

Let me put it another way. If you enjoy your work, you can't be unhappy. No, there are exceptions to that, too. Your wife or husband could have just left you for someone else, or your car radio could have been stolen, or your parrot could have laryngitis, in which case you'd be unhappy no matter how much you love your work.

Let me try again. I'd better decide how to put it, before you tell me where to put it. Okay, here goes. Generally speaking, there's nothing like enjoying your work to make you happy. I think we can all agree on that. It has certainly been true in my case.

For me, show business was always so exciting, so satisfying, so full of laughs and fun that it never seemed like work. And people sense that. Whenever I play Vegas or Lake Tahoe or give a concert they come backstage and tell me I looked like I was really enjoying myself out there. Why shouldn't I enjoy myself? I'm standing there smoking a cigar, hearing myself sing a dozen of my favorite songs in my key, giving a roomful of nice people some laughs and I'm getting paid.

It's all very relaxed, very easy. When I perform I don't sweat. Rodney Dangerfield sweats, Don Rickles sweats, Jackie Gleason sweats. . . . I'm wrong, it's good to sweat.

The next time I'm onstage I'll sweat a little.

I've always said I'd rather be a flop in show business than a success at something I don't like. I'll admit I say it more often now than I did when I was barely making enough to keep that seal I worked with in mackerel. But that's the way I feel about it. I don't think you go into show business just for the money. It's not like selling dresses or making felt hats. You may do very well financially, but that's not what attracted you to it or keeps you in it.

Most of the performers I know would tell you the same thing. Danny Thomas, Bob Hope, Milton Berle, Phyllis Diller, Buddy Hackett, Bob Newhart, Red Buttons, Joan Rivers, Shecky Greene—they all love every minute of it. "The Johnny Carson Show" has been on five nights a week for twenty years, and Johnny still enjoys himself. He should. If you figure the nights he's had guest hosts, he's only been on about a year and three months.

Red Skelton always looked like he was having a blast out there. And I thought he was until I heard he was so nervous he threw up before every performance. Someone once asked Red if it were true that he always did that, and he said, "Sure, doesn't everyone?"

Walter Matthau has a different problem. He loves show business as much as any of us,

Johnny, enjoying his work, too.

and you could hardly be more successful. But like many big stars he's always worrying that it won't last. When we did *The Sunshine Boys* he had just come off three big hits in a row, including *The Odd Couple* with Jack Lemmon. We had a great time making *The Sunshine Boys*, and after we finished the picture Walter and I had lunch together. He'd been out of work maybe three hours. I noticed he was picking at his food, and said, "Walter, you're not eating." He said, "How can I eat? I just spoke to my agent, he's got nothing lined up for me." So I ate his lunch, too.

Actors are the worst of all. Once they get the bug they can't get it out of their system. Ronald Reagan's an exception. He was able to leave acting for politics, even with a smash like *Bedtime for Bonzo* under his belt. Some Democrats would dispute that; not the part about Bonzo, but that he's stopped acting. Personally, I've always liked and admired Ronald Reagan, and I think he's made a great President. In fact, I think he's the best President the Screen Actors Guild ever had.

When Irving Berlin said there's no business like show business he must have been thinking of my end of it. Between the writers, the comedians, the nutty vaudevillians and all the other characters around, you never stop

I told him he'd never amount to anything unless he learned the Time-Step.

laughing. At least I haven't. Let me give you a few small samples of what goes on.

There was this big comedian back in the radio days. He was very funny, very fast on the uptake and an incurable womanizer. I won't tell you his name, but he had his own show every week. I probably could tell you his name, but I won't. The show took place in a New York tavern. Anyway, this comedian got married to a very lovely lady, and the newlyweds immediately went on a honeymoon cruise. And right away, the first night out, he winds up in the cabin of another woman. After a few hours the wife goes looking for him, and sure enough, she bumps into him just as he's coming out of the other woman's cabin. And without batting an eye he says to her, "I forgot to tell you, I'm also a jewel thief."

Then there was the time John Barrymore was riding to his hotel in a cab, and the driver was Jewish. The cabbie said, "Mr. Barrymore, it's an honor for me to have you in my cab. What brings you to New York?" And Barrymore said, "I'm here to play *Hamlet* for the next six weeks." And the cabdriver said, "*Hamlet*? I've seen Jacob P. Adler play *Hamlet*, I've seen Aaron Kessler play *Hamlet*, I've seen Boris Thomashefsky play *Hamlet*. Will they understand it in English?"

Frank Fay was one of our great comedians, and for sarcasm he had no equal. One night he was master of ceremonies at the Mayfair Ball, a very swanky, black-tie affair. Practically every Hollywood star was there, and Fay was in top form. In the middle of one of his lines somebody at one of the tables said something. Fay stopped, looked over in that direction and said, "Who said that?" There was a long silence, then somebody from another table yelled, "Groucho Marx said that!" Fay looked at Groucho and said, "Groucho, why don't you come up here and we'll talk for a few minutes." Groucho just sat there; he wanted no part of Fay. Fay looked right through him and said, "So you do need Zeppo, don't you."

One more story. Look, I'm getting paid by the word. This one's about a comedy writer, John P. Medbury, one of the best. He used to sit in his office and write by the hour. In the little adjoining office was his assistant, a young kid named Harvey Helm. One day Medbury's wife happened to walk into his office while he was out. The top drawer of his desk was open, and she noticed a pair of silk panties. She gingerly held them up, and as Medbury came back into the office, she said, "John, what are these doing in your drawer?"

Without missing a beat, Medbury hollered, "Harvey!" Harvey came in and Medbury said, "You're fired!" I don't think it worked, because the next day when Harvey got to the office he found Medbury sleeping on the couch.

I could go on and on, but that gives you an idea of why I've always gotten such a kick out of show business, and why I could never picture myself in any other profession. It bothers me when I see people who hate what they do for a living, or are bored with it and just go through the motions, getting no pleasure or satisfaction from it.

How do you go to a job every day that you can't stand? The only thing worse would be coming home to a wife you can't stand, or going to a job you can't stand and then coming home to a wife you can't stand.

You'd think someone in this position would do anything to get out of it. But that's seldom the case. People have a way of hanging on to what makes them miserable. At least they know what they've got. The thought of making a change is frightening. What if they can't handle it? What if they fail?

They underestimate themselves and their abilities, and when you think like that you're defeated before you start. Failing once in a

Bally's in Atlantic City. It's a tough job, but somebody has to do it.

while builds character. I should know, I have more character than I know what to do with. For years in the beginning failure was my middle name. It was only the first and the last names I kept changing. I was Harry "Failure" Pierce; I was Joe "Failure" Davis; I was Tom "Failure" Fitzpatrick; and then until I met Gracie I was George "Failure" Burns.

But I never underestimated myself. The audience did that for me. I'd go out on the stage and try something, and if it didn't work, I'd try something else. And when that didn't work I'd try something else. One theater manager suggested I try running an elevator, or running a drill press, or just running.

I shouldn't downgrade other lines of work. Just because something's not for me doesn't mean it's not for someone else. I'm sure there are some people who enjoy selling cemetery lots, although I never knew anyone who enjoyed buying one. As William Shakespeare once said, "How come you can't fill a theater on a Tuesday night?" That doesn't fit, but I figure if I quote Will, the next thing he writes he might quote me.

There was a good point I was about to make . . . oh yes . . . if you're going to accomplish anything worthwhile, you have to be willing to accept a challenge now and then. You can't always play it safe. There are times when you have to take a chance.

When Gracie retired I faced such a time. I had to make a big decision, and I did. I went into show business. Look, when I worked with Gracie, I was retired. I did nothing. We walked on the stage and I said, "Gracie, how's your brother?" and she talked for thirty-eight years.

Now when I suddenly had to go it alone, I didn't know if I could make it. What if they didn't like me alone? What if I didn't like me alone? And then I figured the only way I'd find out was to try it. So I did.

I put a show together for Harrah's at Lake Tahoe, and I wasn't going to take any chances. I surrounded myself with the best: Bobby Darin, the DeCastro Sisters, Brascia & Tybee—they didn't need me. I went out there and I thought I did fine. That night when Gracie and I were in bed, I said, "Gracie, how'd you like the show?"

She said, "Bobby Darin was just fabulous." I waited, and then she said, "The audience just loved the DeCastro Sisters." I waited some more, then she said, "And Brascia and Tybee are the greatest dancing act I've ever seen." I couldn't wait any longer; it was start-ing to get light out. I said, "What did you think of me?" She said, "Bobby Darin was just fabulous."

"Come on, Gracie," I said. "I can take it."

She said, "George, I don't believe that you believe what you're saying. You're reciting all your monologues."

I didn't sleep that night, and can I tell you something, I never recited my monologues again. Now I'm out there on the stage for an hour, just me and my cigar, and it's one of the big pleasures in my life.

It turns out that some of the best things I've done were things I had to be talked into. When they brought me "I Wish I Was 18 Again" and asked me to record it, I thought they were kidding. Who was I to sing country? I can barely sing city. I'm not the country type; I'm from New York's East Side. I don't ride horses, I take cabs.

"The song's not for me," I said. "Give it to Kenny Rogers." They pointed out that it had to be sung by an older man. "Then give it to Kenny Rogers' father," I said.

Irving Fein thought I was crazy; he wanted me to do it. I said, "Nothing could make me do that song." Irving said, "They're not offering you nothing, they're offering you a lot of money." So I took it. It became a hit, and since then I've done several country albums,

That's me playing two parts: God and the Devil.

a TV special from Nashville, and I feel very comfortable with that music. Look, why shouldn't I be a country singer? I'm older than most countries.

Playing "Al Lewis" in *The Sunshine Boys* was another challenge. At the age of seventy-nine I had to become a dramatic actor. The big thing with acting is that you not only have to be able to feel the emotions you are to convey, but you have to feel them when the director yells "Action!"

This gave me trouble until one day it all came to me, and now it's a cinch. If the director wants me to cry, I think of my sex life. If he wants me to laugh, I think of my sex life. And if he wants me to laugh and cry at the same time, I look in the mirror. Olivier has his system, I have mine.

It must have worked, because they gave me an Oscar for *The Sunshine Boys*. But it's the *Oh God!* films that have had the biggest impact. When I go down the street people say, "There's God." They don't say, "There's Al Lewis."

I worried about playing God. We're about the same age, but we grew up in different neighborhoods. It didn't seem right for me to be God. Wouldn't they be better off with someone like Billy Graham? He's taller than I am. Then when they showed me the outfits I'd be wearing for the role, I figured they didn't have any more confidence in me than I did. I was expecting expensive white flowing robes and a halo or two. That stuff I wore must have cost about 12 cents. It looked like God was laying off.

But it worked out great. There was a sequel, and as I write this they're editing the third one, Warner Bros.' *Oh God! You Devil*. This time I've got a dual role. I play God and the Devil. As the Devil I go around with young girls, smoke a lot of cigars and drink martinis. It's the toughest role I ever had to play.

Looking back, I don't know what I would have done if I didn't have my work. And even now I'd be lost without it. People keep asking me when I'm going to retire. They say you're supposed to slow down and take it easy when you get old. Well, when that happens to me I'll think about it. Look, if I had started slowing down when I was sixty-five or seventy, by now I'd be stopped. A turtle would move faster. But I didn't slow down, I kept going. And now at eighty-eight there isn't a turtle around that can pass me.

Not that it matters. In my business the test isn't how fast you move. It's not the Olympics. I have an hour for my stage show, so if it takes a minute or two for me to shuffle out there, who cares? In fact, the longer it takes the more they applaud. They're pulling for me to make it to the center of the stage. So that's no problem. And when I record a country album I can do it sitting down. And if they want me to do a tap dance in a movie, they hire a double and I'm still sitting down.

So if I still love my work and I can still do it, why retire, especially now that I have it both ways? Not only am I making movies at eighty-eight, but as a senior citizen I only pay half price to see myself up there on the screen. I'd have to be crazy to retire. I'll never quit. I'm going to stay in show business until I'm the only one left.

XI

. . . and in Conclusion

WHEN I STARTED this book the very first thing I did was asked myself, "What is it that makes me happy?" After thinking about it I realized there are a lot of things that make me happy, which is good because I'd hate to have all my happiness in one basket.

As I explained in the last chapter, my work makes me happy. Being in reasonably good health for a man my age, or for that matter a woman my age, makes me happy. Cathy Carr makes me happy. Getting the most out of a tough bridge hand makes me happy. And I must admit a standing ovation makes me happy. Let's face it, a pat on the back is nice, providing the guy who does the patting isn't Larry Holmes.

I'd be lying if I told you I haven't enjoyed all the attention I've received, especially in recent years. The public has been very good to me, and it's not a one-way romance. If my fans appreciate me, I appreciate them just as much.

I've never understood why some performers resent their fans. What do they want, people who can't stand them? I've had both and I'll take the fans anytime. Those stars worry about going into a restaurant and having everyone notice them. They should eat at home. To me the time to worry is when you're in a restaurant and they don't notice you.

I don't mind it at all if they come over to my table while I'm eating dinner and ask for my autograph. I'll sign anything: napkins, menus, ties, just as long as it isn't the check. When that comes I ask Irving Fein for his autograph.

If a little kid comes to me and calls me "God," what am I going to do, tell him to get lost? I'm too busy to say hello? I've got to go, I'm running behind on my miracles for the day? Would God do that? Of course not! I smile, offer the kid a cigar, make his father pay me for it and the three of us are happy.

You know something, I should ask my fans for their autographs. Sometimes they're funnier than I am, like when they mistake me for someone else. That's always happening. I never tell them they're wrong, I go along with it. It started when I worked with Gracie. Half the time they called me Mr. Allen. I didn't mind, Allen got all the laughs. It would have been worse if they had called me Mr. Smith or Mr. Dale. At least they got the right team.

One time a woman mistook me for Fred Allen. She asked me how my wife, Portland, was. I said, "She's fine, great little cook." She said, "It's amazing—you look the same in person. But how come you're not talking through your nose?" I said, "I only do that when I get paid."

I've even been mistaken for Bob Burns, the comedian who made the bazooka famous on the Bing Crosby radio show. This fellow came up to me and said, "Mr. Burns, I never miss you, you're my favorite. When are you going to play the bazooka again?"

Now Bob Burns had been dead for twenty-nine years, but I didn't want to tell him that. So I said, "I'm glad you reminded me. I haven't touched my bazooka in years, but as soon as I get home I'll take it out and try it."

You won't believe this, but once I was actually mistaken for Burt Reynolds. Last year I was in the lobby of the Sherry-Netherland hotel in New York, and some guy said to me, "Hey, Burt, are you still going around with Loni Anderson?" I said, "No, I'm dancing with Sally Fields again." How could he think I was Burt Reynolds? It's ridiculous. Burt's got black hair, mine is gray.

The one that tops all of these I think I've told before, but it's worth repeating. I was sitting in a doctor's office, and there was a lady sitting next to me. She said, "It's exciting to be sitting in a waiting room with a great celebrity." I said, "It certainly is. Who are you?"

She laughed and said, "I know who you are, Mr. Benny." "Thanks," I said. "Everybody recognizes me."

"How's Mary?"

"She was fine when I left her in bed this morning."

She said, "Is it true everything George Burns says makes you laugh?"

"Oh yes, he's a scream," I said. "He's the funniest man I ever met."

Then the nurse came in and said to me, "Mr. Burns, the doctor's ready to see you now." The woman looked at me, and said, "Are you George Burns?"

"That's right."

"What were you doing in bed with Mary this morning?" she asked. I said, "At our age it takes both of us to keep her warm."

Some of the fans do strange things. I got a letter four or five months ago from a fan in Oklahoma City. He said his grandfather had seen Burns & Allen in vaudeville, then his father and mother listened to us on radio and he watched us on television, had seen all my movies, read all my books, saw all my TV specials and even had all my albums.

Then he wrote, "I'm getting married March twenty-fourth, and since I'm your biggest fan the least you can do is send us a nice sports car for a present. We'd prefer a Chevrolet Corvette, but if that's too expensive, a Pontiac Firebird will do—any color but yellow."

I didn't know what to do. I thought and thought about it, and I finally sent him a picture of myself and wished them a wonderful marriage and signed my name. I haven't heard from him since. Maybe he's not my biggest fan anymore.

I get all kinds of requests. After the first *Oh God!* picture came out I received a letter at my home from Milwaukee. It was addressed "God—Beverly Hills." It was from a six-year-old boy. It started out: "Dear Mr. God. I know you're very busy, but I have a big favor to ask. This Sunday is our championship baseball game, and I would be very happy if you would make it not rain. Don't forget, it's this Sunday." I guess it didn't rain, because I got another letter from that boy. It said, "Thanks, but we lost."

You never know when you're going to meet

a fan. One morning I was driving to my office the same way I've been doing for years. I had to cross a busy intersection just before I got there, and I was almost through it when a guy ran a red light and smashed into the passenger side of my car. The car was a mess, but fortunately I was just shaken up. I got out and asked him what he thought he was doing, running a red light like that. He said, "You're George Burns." I said, "I almost wasn't." Then he told me what a great fan he was and how he loved everything I did. I said, "If you're such a big fan, why did you try to kill me?"

By then the police had arrived, and he started telling them what a big fan he was. After the police wrote out the report they took a picture of the two cars, and the guy said to them, "Would you mind getting one of George and me together? Is it okay with you, George?"

I said, "All right, just don't kiss me."

Another time I was at NBC on my way to do "The Johnny Carson Show" and a woman stopped me. She said, "You're George Burns, aren't you?" I said, "That's right." "I can't believe it," she said. "This is the first time I've ever seen you alive." I hope she wasn't disappointed.

Sometimes they get so excited they don't realize what they're saying. I don't know how many times I've had someone point their finger at me and say, "You're you, aren't you?" I say, "Yes," and they say, "I can't believe you're really you." I try to calm them down by saying, "Look, I've been 'you' for years."

Some people come up and test me. They say, "Do you know who you are?" I say, "Give me a minute, I have to think about it."

This one is really a beauty. After my last TV special a woman rushed up to me the next day and said, "Mr. Burns, I saw your special last night." I said, "Thank you," and she continued with, "And I spoke to my sister in St. Louis and she saw it, too!"

I said, "That's very flattering," and she said, "Just imagine, I'm in Los Angeles and she's in St. Louis and we both saw the same thing. Isn't television amazing! What a world we live in!"

I thanked her again, why I don't know. All she did was compliment her television set.

And fans love to take pictures, especially at airports. I'll be sitting there waiting for my flight, and someone will rush over to me with a camera, put a baby in my lap and say, "Mr. Burns, do you mind smiling?" I must have had hundreds of pictures taken with babies. I

With my writers Hal and Harvey. I taught them everything they know.

don't dare travel unless I carry two or three extra pair of pants.

Here's a compliment I'll never forget. I was playing the Riviera Hotel in Las Vegas, and one day during lunch this attractive young couple came up to the table. The girl said, "Mr. Burns, we're on our honeymoon, and meeting you is the most exciting thing that's happened to us." Now that's what I call a fan.

Look, they may not always realize exactly what they're saying, but I love my fans. I'm grateful for every one of them.

Speaking of being grateful, it's time to thank the two fellows who helped me write this book. I know it's time for that, because they just told me. Contrary to the picture of them standing with me, they don't smoke cigars. They don't smoke at all. They put up with my cigars and I put up with their jokes.

The oldest is Hal Goldman and the youngest one is Harvey Berger. Actually, I'm the oldest. I'm older than both of them put together, and they can throw in their agents, too. Hal's an old hand in the business; he's forgotten more about comedy than most writers know. In fact, if he forgets any more, I may never be able to use him again. The other kid is a relative newcomer. He came into my office two years ago and couldn't write his

With my secretary, Jack Langdon, in the middle, and Eric Butler— whatever he does.

My manager, Irving Fein, telling me he renewed me for another year.

own name. But after sitting at my feet for two years he can now write it easily. Look, if these kids don't learn, I don't keep them.

I also have to thank Jack Langdon, my secretary. I was going to say some glowing things about him, but he just asked for a raise, so that's the end of this paragraph.

Eric Butler is a new kid who's working for me. He's only been with me nine months, so I haven't had a chance to find out what he does.

Also, I should mention Cindy Delpit, Liz Slusher, Rieneke, Lori Garland and Tina Littlewood, the five models who posed for the pictures in this book. I want to thank them for being so beautiful and cooperative. If I were a little younger, I might have more to thank them for.

Most of the pictures in the book were taken by that fine photographer, Peter Borsari. I wanted you to see what he looked like, but he doesn't have a picture of himself.

I mustn't forget my literary agents, Arthur and Richard Pine, who deserve credit for coming up with the idea for this book. Next time I'll come up with the idea and they can write the book.

Again I want to thank Phyllis Grann, my editor and publisher, who has great editorial judgment, impeccable taste, unfailing literary instincts and dances close.

And now I come to my personal manager, Irving Fein. I appreciate the invaluable help Irving has given me, not just with this book but with everything I've been doing. He's my idea of what a good manager should be. Not only has he a good head for business, but when it comes to charity and giving, his heart is in the right place. I can't think of a single worthy cause he hasn't insisted I contribute to.

I'm also grateful to (in alphabetical order): Steve Allen, Milton Berle, Red Buttons, Johnny Carson, Jack Carter, Carol Channing, Phyllis Diller, Bob Hope, Walter Matthau, Bob Newhart, Don Rickles, Joan Rivers and Danny Thomas for those flattering comments about your author. It wasn't really necessary to mention them individually, but I'm still getting paid by the word.

One Last Definition of Happiness

Happiness is finally getting to write these two words—

THE END

After writing a book a man has to relax.

The publishers hope that this
Large Print Book has brought
you pleasurable reading.
Each title is designed to make
the text as easy to see as possible.
G. K. Hall Large Print Books are
available from your library and
your local bookstore. Or you can
receive information on upcoming
and current Large Print Books by
mail and order directly from the
publisher. Just send your name
and address to:

G. K. Hall & Co.
70 Lincoln Street
Boston, Mass. 02111

or call, toll-free:

1-800-343-2806

A note on the text
Large print edition designed by
Fred Welden.
Composed in 18 pt Plantin
on a Mergenthaler 202
by Compset Inc., Beverly MA.